T0398243

Starting Inquiry-based Science in the Early Years

Young children are intuitive scientists. This book builds on their inherent curiosity and problem solving as they move forward in their scientific thinking. Science develops from early beginnings and a solid foundation in the early years is essential for their future learning and engagement with the subject. *Starting Inquiry-based Science in the Early Years* shows you how you can support children's emerging scientific skills by working with them and scaffolding their inquiries as they experiment, hypothesise and investigate, building on their natural curiosity.

Full of practical advice, it offers a wide range of scientific activities that can be carried out in partnership with young children. Each activity presents a challenge for the child to solve by thinking and talking through their ideas and then carrying out their own investigations. This invaluable guide focuses on helping children to follow their own line of inquiry and supporting them in mastering the skills and vocabulary they need in order to do this. Features include:

- an explanation of the key skills children need to acquire and practical ideas for developing these;
- useful lists of relevant vocabulary and everyday resources;
- cue questions to encourage children's thinking skills;
- cross-curricular links to show how the activities support early literacy and mathematics.

Providing a rich bank of resources for promoting scientific experiences and learning, this highly practical book will help you ensure that the children in your care have the strong foundations they need to become confident, successful scientists in the future.

Sue Dale Tunnicliffe is a Reader in Science Education at the University College London, Institute of Education, UK.

Starting Inquiry-based Science in the Early Years

Look, talk, think and do

Sue Dale Tunnicliffe

Routledge
Taylor & Francis Group

LONDON AND NEW YORK

First published 2015
by Routledge
2 Park Square, Milton Park, Abingdon, Oxon OX14 4RN

and by Routledge
711 Third Avenue, New York, NY 10017

Routledge is an imprint of the Taylor & Francis Group, an informa
business

British Library Cataloguing in Publication Data
A catalogue record for this book is available from the British Library

Library of Congress Cataloging in Publication Data
Tunnicliffe, Sue Dale.
  Starting inquiry-based science in the early years : look, talk, think
  and do / Sue Dale Tunnicliffe.
    pages cm
  Includes bibliographical references and index.
  ISBN 978-1-138-77855-9 (alk. paper) — ISBN 978-1-138-77856-6
  (pbk : alk. paper) — ISBN 978-1-315-77190-8 (ebk)
  1. Science—Study and teaching (Early childhood)
  2. Science—Study and teaching (Preschool)   I. Title.
  LB1139.5.S35T85 2016
  372.35'044—dc23   2015004369

ISBN: 978-1-138-77855-9 (hbk)
ISBN: 978-1-138-77856-6 (pbk)
ISBN: 978-1-315-77190-8 (ebk)

Typeset in Bembo
by Keystroke, Station Road, Codsall, Wolverhampton

For Richard, who inquired

And his children, Daniel, Luc and Josh, who are still inquiring

Contents

Preface

This book is written particularly in mind for adults working one to one or with a few children. I have found that many adults in this position want to help these emergent scientists develop their scientific skills, knowledge and understanding, but often are unsure as to how to go about this, particularly when the child is noticing something inside or outside, which has caught their interest and is investigating. Most of us are then tempted to recall science facts from our own school days.

I have come to realise that having a dialogue with the child about a situation, starting with questions, is a very effective means of beginning a positive conversation. This book provides an introduction to topics that children encounter, together with some examples of children's responses to some situations relevant to the chapter topic and then some cue questions to encourage the emergent scientist in their investigation. Each chapter gives some of the things or 'equipment' you need to pursue the challenges if you want to set up the opportunity for an investigation, as well as vocabulary and dialogue in the form of questions or challenges to initiate the dialogue and can be usefully employed to enhance the child's vocabulary.

The first chapter is an introduction to the rest of the book. The second chapter provides an introduction to some theories about observed children at play and their actions, whilst the third chapter considers some ways of recording a child's observations, actions and progress, for those of you who want to keep a record or are required to do so by where you meet and work with young children. The remaining chapters focus on various themes and include examples of some children's interpretation of incidences within these themes, as well as suggestions for initial dialogue leading into inquiry with an emergent scientist or groups of them.

I am particularly indebted to Elizabeth Myers, a former student of mine and an excellent early years practitioner, who has provided invaluable informed advice in the writing of this book. Of course, I must acknowledge the input generations of emergent scientists have made to my understanding of how children engage in science from their earliest years, many of whose responses to an experience are included in the book. In particular, I acknowledge the contribution made by my own children and grandsons.

Chapter 1

Introduction: format of the book

This book focuses on structured partnership activity between an adult and an early learner, but with a difference. The objective is to use a particular approach of posing a challenge via a cue question to the child. This is not only to provide a stimulus for them to explore their own designed science experience but to scaffold the thinking of a participating child through further questions and often with the outcome in the initial question. For example, "Is the moon always visible at night?" whereby the child has to plan a strategy to answer the question. Children have to learn certain skills first of all and then hone them with practice and learn to see where they can apply these skills, of thought and actions, to a new situation. The partner can assist them in this learning with the appropriate cue as they master the skill or work out their thoughts. This is difficult to do but try. Bear in mind the words of the Russian psychologist Vygotsky, "What a child can do with assistance today she will be able to do by herself tomorrow" (1987, p.87).

The activities in the book provide not only a starting point but also often a finishing outcome and the child has to work out how to proceed from the start to the outcome. Talking to the learner as s/he progresses in planning and doing the actions to meet the challenge can reveal much about the previous knowledge and experience of the learner and their ability to verbalise their thoughts and skills at problem solving. Using open questions and 'push back' questions (Chin, 2007) can prompt the child further in developing their thinking and reasoning.

The partner adult often needs to set up the items to show the starting point and the end point when they want to create a learning opportunity. Thus, in the case of the magnet activity discussed in Chapter 2, the start would be a pile of wrapped items and the end point would be selecting one wrapped item from a pile of other wrapped items. The one item could be labelled 'magnet' and the child told it is a magnet. In the case of some studies, e.g. on weather, photographs of an end point might be used, or of a starting point to stimulate looking, talking, thinking and doing. Thus learners are encouraged to work out how they can use the starting point and reach the given outcome. In this partnership activity (which is not fully structured) because you are encouraging their thinking by asking cue questions as appropriate and introducing appropriate cue questions, you should not tell them what to do. The relevant vocabulary is provided, as well as the skills and experiences they need before they can tackle the given activity.

Specific instructions to achieve the outcome are not given, rather the emergent scientist will need to think and do the investigation as they see fit, with some teacher-led cue questions, provided during activities. It is envisaged that the activities and dialogue are conducted one to one or adult to several learners. However, an adult can adapt the strategies for their own purposes and the whole activity should s/he wish.

Each chapter starts with an introduction followed by children's real ideas about the topic. These are very short case histories of children with whom I have worked and their responses in investigations or challenges about the topic of the chapter.

The aims of the activities follow and should you have to write learning plans when working with children these can be useful for initial, overall planning and monitoring of a child's learning. A list of vocabulary that can be used when adults are working with these learners is included, which some adults have found very useful in assessing progress. Before an investigation can really be carried out there are certain skills that a learner needs, such as being able to pick up items, pour water, and such foundation experiences are given so you can ensure that the learner has such skills. In a planned learning situation it is useful to have things to use in investigations available so a list of possibly useful items is included. After the introductory three chapters actual activities or challenges are suggested, in particular topics that in my experience interest early learners: ourselves, other animals, plants and fungi, pushes and pulls, changes and outside. Each activity is introduced with a start or cue question for the adult to use to start the investigative process. Additionally some 'throw back' questions prompt the learner to the next move. We don't tell them or show them; many of us find this difficult. Please try and suggest further action through dialogue. Finally, a brief summary of expected outcomes is given.

Assessment may be an important part of your work so assessment suggestions and record charts are provided, as well as suggestions for recording in some form if this is a feature of your work.

References

Chin, C. (2007) Teacher Questioning in Science Classrooms: Approaches that Stimulate Productive Thinking. *Journal of Research in Science Teaching.* 44(6) 815–843.

Vygotsky, L. (1987) *Mind in Society.* Cambridge, MA, Harvard University Press, p. 87.

Chapter 2

Observations and actions – play: starting learning science

Introduction

Learning science begins with babies looking around, gradually acquiring manipulative skills they can use for a definite action and then play. Learning is gradual and begins with intuitive ideas but is consolidated by noticing a phenomenon, talking about it, and thinking about it again and investigating where appropriate and sharing with someone else. Learning does not occur in a linear manner but in a constructive way, sometimes referred to as a spiral curriculum context, being developed increasingly in more depth (Bruner, 1977). The starting point for science is observation (Sylva et al., 1980). We strive as educators to encourage young children and their associated adults, parents, relatives, other carers and teachers, to share their observations, talk about them and increase their own self-esteem and literacy. Moreover, children are intuitive scientists (Gopnik, 2009).

> Children, we now know, need to talk, and to experience a rich diet of spoken language in order to think and learn. Reading, writing and number may be acknowledged as curriculum 'basics' but talk is the true foundation for teaching.
> (Alexander, 2008, p. 9)

However, when engrossed in activity children do not necessarily talk. Very young children who play do not talk, but they do play and investigate whilst they play. When being involved in imaginative activities, they might tell the story out loud of what, for instance, their Lego figures or toy cars or dolls are doing and provide an oral narrative. On other occasions when they are involved in observations and investigations they often do not talk (Tizard and Hughes, 1984); sometimes they say a statement out loud that is really a hidden question.

Furthermore, it is now accepted that there is an intimate link between language and thought and thus the cognitive development of a child is affected to a considerable extent by the nature, context and forms of language, which s/he hears and uses (Halliday, 1993). We now recognise that play is crucial to the development of a child (Moyles, 1989) and that society should promote awareness of and work to change the attitudes towards play. Whitbread at al. (2012) point out that play is the work of children and essential for intellectual achievement and emotional wellbeing. Learning through experience is developed in both spontaneous and directed play and introducing inquiry-based science fits well into extended play activities progressing to challenges to solve. Play, after all, is often very much problem solving (Moyles, 1989). 'Just playing', is a phrase that has been used in a derogatory sense by educators, and some parents and other adults, unfamiliar with early years learners. Parents who recollect their own education assume this is how it should be for all as their own usually secondary stage experience means they fail to understand the essential and critical values that link a child's learning through play.

The starting point for the learning of science and engineering, at this early age, is play. As such these early learners are making observations and asking questions, albeit to themselves and devising their own strategies for eliciting an answer. Such working out by the child is them asking themselves hidden questions even though in the earliest years their thoughts are not verbalised. The only evidence we, as observers, have is we can see the actions of the children, which are thus the expressed model of their science investigation. Moreover, such learning occurs in the immediate environment of the child, in his/her community, with the people with whom s/he spends their time, and begins long before any formal educational interaction. Starting children on their path in learning science as in other subjects is a community endeavour. These places of potential learning are where they live and the immediate environment outside. In these locations children witness everyday activities such as cooking, cleaning, washing, various activities with materials such as textiles, wood, clay, as well as identifying and being involved with basic life processes such as moving, breathing, eating, excreting and the human activities associated with the life processes and beyond. Children are immersed in their environment, including natural structures or built, human constructs such as their village or adjacent areas, which all contain various amounts of technology, maths and science. This can range from a simple cooking vessel being used on an open fire to mobile phones; from natural vegetation to a manicured garden and the everyday non-built areas. Moreover, the natural environment comprises physical, geological and biological matter, and features of this, such as rocks, plants and watercourses, may be observed. Additionally, the culture and particular uses of science and technology by the community with whom the children live are evident and noticed, pointed out by members of the community, for instance, buildings, transport and water sources.

As children acquire early language they begin to label phenomena. This naming is an inherent human need (Bruner, Goodnow and Austin, 1956; Markman, 1989). Additionally, young children ask questions incessantly when given the opportunity (Tough, 1977), a behaviour that often disappears in the formal education environment where class triadic dialogue takes over. In order to talk and express themselves, children will need to know the relevant vocabulary. If they do not know the word they will use the 'nearest fit'. My eldest grandson noticed the reflections of trees on the flat surface of a body of water, across which a boat was passing. He remarked on the *shadows* of the trees, not knowing the word 'reflection'. In England a curriculum for the early years is laid out in a government document (DfE, 2012).

Becoming an emergent scientist

Children learn their science as they learn about the phenomena in the world in which they live. Emergent scientists acquire the necessary basic concepts to enable them to become participant inquirers in science through active involvement with their everyday environment and the adults around them. This gives the learners experiences and provides opportunities for them to acquire experiences, whilst you introduce skills and vocabulary. But when children construct understanding for themselves it is their understanding of their world. It is salutary for we educators to bear in mind when considering formal teaching strategies for very young children to learn more about science that school science generally assumes that, for any scientific issue, there is a single valid scientific conception, so that other ideas that do not agree with it are alternative conceptions, often called misconceptions. Personal knowledge that has been acquired through the child's own life experiences, both real and virtual, are referred to by Driver et al. (1985) as alternative conceptions. They are, after all, what the child thinks and they are unaware that their interpretation and idea do not match that of accepted science; to them, the scientists' idea is a misconception! However, concepts or ideas recognised by the scientific community are the units of knowledge that formal education requires children to grasp. Such core shared understanding, enables people to arrange and group, and thus categorise information. In their early years, if provided with opportunities, these early learners actively develop essential concepts and acquire the skills and processes through experience.

The process of acquiring such an essential foundation has, in my observation and experience, different stages in science experiences for learners. Firstly there is the *personal, spontaneous* science, then a *partnership* and finally the more formal or *designed experiences*. Children observe and try an action, such as Luc looking at a toy slide winding downwards in a spiral then, with no prompt from anyone, releasing a small ball down the ramp, again and again. These personal learners intuitively match items one to one and make correlations.

Early years children match one item to another, a one-to-one correspondence. They group items into categories, which they define or classify. For example, all red shapes and all blue shapes might be grouped together, or all vehicles with wheels referred to as 'dig digs'. The young emergent 'scientist' delights in finding they can make marks in the sand or dirt with a stick, or make noises by hitting an object with another. They delight in measuring, emptying and filling containers, pouring water from one container to another and back again, and they enjoy controlling things. Watch a child sit with a switch and push it on and then off, and then on and then off, or pulling a balloon on a string down and letting it float up again, saying, "Up", and then, "Down!" as they repeat the action, again and again!

Children find items to play with. A small boy I noticed sitting on a veranda in Sreepur Village, Bangladesh, had a small collection of pebbles, which he threw in the air, in turn caught, then placed them together in sets according to their size. These children do not have developed world toys to play with but investigate through play with everyday items.

Three categories of early science interactions

Learning science in the beginning is a solo occupation of personal observation and experimentation. It can also be a partnership of exploring a phenomenon, first noticed by the learner and amplified by the facilitator, the accompanying adult, or indeed pointed out by the facilitator and explored together with key cue questions. This sort of 'recipe' approach requires little thinking of the experimenter who follows instructions. Instead of telling the child they can see what science, e.g. a force, is being shown in the action adults should let the child find out by experience, not tell them first. However, if the recipe is not given, thinking is involved! Midway between, is perhaps a partnership of thinking, with a recognised starting point and the outcome, but the pathway of reaching the outcome from the starting point has to be worked out! Such is the basis for the role of the adult in this book. Children are creative thinkers. Recent research by Robson (2014) has developed an approach that she refers to as the ACCT framework (Analysing Children's Creative Thinking) to identify and also analyse this in young children.

Young children

We must, however, be realistic and remember that a learner has to acquire the skills needed to carry out investigations before they can focus on inquiry alone. They cannot focus on inquiry if they are also struggling with the technique of using items. Thus early learners often need some play to find out how things work and this is so important in their development, as, in later years of formal schooling we need to teach the techniques before posing a challenge, rather like instructing an adult in how to drive a car before letting them loose on the road unsupervised. Practice does indeed make perfect in this sense.

Spontaneous, unprompted

A spontaneous experience is when the child notices something independently. Nicholas noticed that every time he dropped something from his high chair it went to the floor, and someone picked it up and returned it to him, whereupon be repeated the action! Every time the item fell to the floor, the child was observing, gathering data and experiencing a pattern of events. Data! The child was being an intuitive scientist (Gopnik, 2009). Finlay, a child who played with two similar-shaped magnets, showed me that they push each other away; they were stronger than he was! Try as he might, he could not push them together. The force of the two magnets pushing away was greater than him. He was impressed.

Partnership experiences

The adult initiates a potential learning experience through setting a scenario. Such scenarios are suggested in this book. Alternatively, the adult provides a learning opportunity by noticing an event or phenomenon when with a child and assigns a relevant question, often thus directing the child with a pertinent question or comment to try a particular line of action. These experiences are not pre-planned. They occur when the adult's experience or intuition or both indicate that this is an opportune moment to develop skills, actions and vocabulary. An example follows.

Josh and Luc, both four years old, went into the garden where there was a paving stone lying on the grass. I suggested that we look under the stone as I wondered what might be there. I, of course, already knew! We lifted the stone, and with the stone up and safely leant against the wall, the boys were excited to notice that the grass was not green like the rest of the grass plants forming the lawn, but yellow. As the facilitating adult I could ask them why they thought this was, and guide them to the thought that no light could reach the grass under the stone, whilst the lawn grass had access to the sunlight. This activity wasn't planned but happened. Had I wanted to help the children realise that plants need light to be green, I could have walked with them outside and found the stone and begun a dialogue encouraging them to inquire. However, this investigation was initiated by them but developed by me as a learning partner!

Structured learning experiences

Structured experiences are preplanned activities that can occur in many different ways or when an adult recognizes an opportunity for a science activity and initiates it from a situation.

If you perform a demonstration for children to show them a phenomenon, like making bubbles with soapsuds or blowing up a balloon and letting it go, you are providing a structured experience. Many school science lessons (and cookery ones) are of this nature, when an investigation is planned for the child to carry out. Helping children to acquire the necessary fundamental science skills that they need to be able to be intrusive, emergent scientists by themselves, such as pouring, or building stable towers, are structured instructional activities.

Parents and carers and particularly teachers of early years learners sometimes set up structured experiences. Such set-ups are designed and instigated when the adult has a definite experience that they want to introduce to the children, such as planting seeds so the learners observe what happens when they grow, or finding out which items are attracted to magnets.

In these three types of early science opportunities the vocabulary used and the form of dialogue are of paramount importance.

CASE STUDY

Case study I – magnets with Josh (5 years 6 months)

I had a collection of everyday objects, such as a coin, paper clip, pebble, marble, eraser and wrapped sweet, covered in wrapping paper in a box or party bag on the table in the kitchen. I knew one of them was a magnet but I could not work out which one it was because I could not see through the paper, in case that gave me a clue. Josh came by and asked what I had and what I was doing. I said that somewhere in the collection of objects there was a magnet and I had to find it.

The child's ideas

I assumed that Josh knew what a magnet is and what it can do, an unrealistic assumption on my part. He recognised the word but only had a very limited understanding of its properties. I should have done pre-investigation work with him first. It is so important to ensure that a child has previous relevant experience or has the opportunity, in this exemplar, to have played with magnets or seen them at home.

(continued)

(continued)

> The following dialogue occurred:
>
> ME: "What is a magnet? What can it do?"
> JOSH: "Sticks to metal."
> ME: "I need to find which of these things is a magnet. How could we find out which is the magnet wrapped up in this box of other things?"
> JOSH: "I don't know."
> *He tipped the wrapped items out of the box and arranged them on the table.*
> ME: "How can we find out?"
> *Josh explored the items, feeling them. He touched all the wrapped up items.*
> JOSH: "I think I know. I'm going to stick them all on the fridge." *He proceeded to do so.*
> "No these don't stick to the fridge . . . magnets should." *Family have a collection of fridge magnets on the metal door.* "That does." *He found two things that stuck onto the fridge door.*
> ME: "Why? Would sticking things be magnets?"
> JOSH: "I didn't know that magnets stuck to fridges and other things."
>
> Some early foundation magnet activities are suggested in Chapter 8 Pushes and pulls.

Using words, listening to children's ideas, experiences and understanding and asking cue questions

In order to facilitate structured learning experiences, you will need to be alert to word meanings used by these young children, as words will mean one thing to one person and something else to another. When I was trying out this activity with 4-year-olds in a group, one girl just kept saying, "Garage". Eventually, it transpired that her family's fridge, with a metal door, was in the garage. Another 3-year-old girl in an early years' setting, knew that magnets 'stuck on fridges' – she told me so! She took the items from my wrapped collection on the table, picking them up one by one, and tried to stick them onto the play wooden fridge. But no success. She found they did not stick. This perplexed her. This item was called a 'fridge'. However, I knew what she did not; it is not the name of the 'fridge' that means it has the property that causes the magnet to adhere to the surface, it is the material from which is made. The so-called 'fridge' was a replica made of wood. Only real working 'fridges' with metal doors hold magnets fast!

The activity described above was a partnership activity, whereas the activity described below was planned as a structured activity but developed into a partnership. The teacher set up the activity but the children ignored the directions, instead taking on the activity in their way and leading their inquiry.

The class teacher had discussed the activity previously. She had worked out a curriculum rationale of using different shapes on a string, which linked to previous maths work. She had also identified appropriate equipment, as the equipment suggested was not part of the school equipment. We used clamps and stands as the equipment to attach the string and blobs. We also used yoghurt containers as the skittles.

The teacher trialled it by working with several groups; the children observed the activity and they captured the data. She worked initially with four children and found that was too many; she then tried a group of three and found that one child was isolated. She concluded that two was the ideal number.

The dialogue was recorded and transcribed. A sample is shown below:

TEACHER: "Where shall we put them (skittles)?"
BOY: "At the back."
TEACHER: "What about the rope, what can we do?"
GIRL: "Like this."
TEACHER: "That's a good idea, you do your plan."
GIRL: "Could also does it, like this *(she proceeded to demonstrate)*."
TEACHER: "What ways make it different? Make it more of a challenge?"
GIRL: "Do it *(she patted the string)* at the side . . . like that."
BOY: "We could get another bottle."
TEACHER: "What makes it a good swing?"
GIRL: "It's a bit like playing bat and ball."
TEACHER: "What makes it so good?"

So what? The use of questions

It is all very well observing and listening to learning situations but what can they tell us? In this case the transcript was then read and reread to identify the categories according to a categorisation, first worked out by a researcher called Christine Chin, in Singapore (Chin, 2007).

The transcript was analysed, read and reread, looking at the technique and the questions identified. There were twenty-five items identified in this transcript. Each question was then matched with a category of Chin's questioning. The results are shown in Table 2.1:

The largest category of questions used by the teacher in scaffolding the progress of the learners in this activity was of a Socratic form; of which the Socratic challenge was the focus of over three-quarters of the questions. However, where appropriate, the teacher was engaged in verbal 'throw back' and 'reflective toss', whereby the child's response to a first question is answered with a question or 'reflective toss' manoeuvre. When appropriate the early years' teacher framed questions.

These children were 5 years old; they did not understand the word 'science' but they used their own experience and skills in a true inquiry-based science manner, to meet the challenge they had been set. They took ownership of the activity and did not follow the proscribed sequence given in the activity by the project. Children at this stage in English early years' classes are used to problem solving and using their own experiences. The message from this study is for teachers to utilise free exploring in the learning environment and to be flexible, encouraging the children to use their existing knowledge, skills and experience in solving problems and meeting challenges.

Technical language is not introduced except where appropriate. The activity was modified by the teacher, alert to the development of these children as emergent

Table 2.1 The number and categories of questions generated in the swing game

Main categories of questioning (From Chin, 2007)	No. N=25	Subordinate category of questioning	No
Socratic questioning	20		
		Pumping	4
		Reflective toss	4
		Constructive challenge	12
Semantic tapestry	2		
		Focusing and zooming	2
Framing question	3		
		Question-based prelude	2
		Question-based summary	1
	25		

scientists rather than instructed, guided partners. Activities should aim to: a) use equipment that is available; b) fit into the curriculum plan if working in a formal setting such as nursery; c) suit the children who are following the activity.

Summary

The key to starting science is for the adults to observe the child and provide suitable cues for them to develop their ideas and questions. It is essential to understand their use of words, as their meaning may not be the same as that of the adult. It is essential not to tell the children what to do but to scaffold the activity with appropriate questions and actions. Recognition of the different types of questions that may be used is invaluable, as well as recognising the very basic idea that the learner is exploring and the further scientific knowledge and understanding such an investigation can lead to, but without telling the child.

References

Alexander, R. (2008) *Towards Dialogic Teaching: Rethinking Classroom Talk*. Cambridge, Dialogos, York.
Bruner, J. (1977) *The Process of Education*. Cambridge, MA, Harvard University Press, Revised edition.
Bruner, J. S., Goodnow, J. J. and Austin, G. A. (1956) *A Study of Thinking*. New York, John Wiley, Science Editions, Inc.
Chin, C. (2007) Teacher Questioning in Science Classrooms: Approaches that Stimulate Productive Thinking. *Journal of Research in Science Teaching*. 44(6) 815–843.
DfE (2012) *Statutory Framework for the Early Years Foundation Stage. Setting the Standards for Learning, Development and Care for Children from Birth to Five*. London, DfE.

Driver, R. Guesne, E. and Tiberghien, A. (1985) *Children's Ideas in Science*. Buckingham, Open University Press.

Gopnik, A. (2009) *The Philosophical Baby: What Children's Minds Tell Us About Truth, Love, and the Meaning of Life*. New York, USA, Farrar, Straus and Giroux.

Halliday, M. A. K. (1993) Towards a Language-based Theory of Education. *Linguistics in Education* 5.

Markman, E. (1989) *Categorization and Naming in Children: Problems of Induction*. Cambridge, MA, The MIT Press.

Moyles, J. (1989) *Just Playing? The Role and Status of Play in Early Childhood Education*. Maidenhead, Open University Press.

Robson, S. (2014) The Analysing Children's Creative Thinking Framework: Development of an Observational Led Approach to Identifying and Analysing Young Children's Creative Thinking. *British Educational Research Journal*. 40 (1) 121–14.

Sylva, K., Roy, C. and Painter, M. (1980) *Child Watching at Playgroup and Nursery School*. London, Grant McIntyre.

Tizard, R. and Hughes, M. (1984) *Young Children Learning: Talking and Thinking at Home and at School*. London, Fontana.

Tough, J. (1977) *The Development of Meaning*. London, George Allen and Unwin.

Whitbread, D., Basilio, M., Kuvalja, M. and Verma, M. (2012) *The Importance of Play: A Report on the Value of Children's Play with a Series of Policy Recommendations*. Brussels, Belgium, Toys Industries for Europe.

Chapter 3

Starting science, recording and assessing early investigations

Introduction

Most people who encounter young learners and who are interested in their learning monitor through observation of actions as a child plays and interacts with their surroundings – what they notice, do and achieve. Through such observations adults may notice and remark on the achievements of the learner. By talking and listening to children who can verbalise their thoughts, ask questions and compose their own narratives, adults may understand even more how the child is progressing in terms of skills and understanding. Adults working formally with young learners may have to record such achievements for a variety of recording and reporting requirements. This chapter discusses ways in which you can monitor and record progress, such as keeping a photo journal (Katz, 2012) and ways of involving children in activities that could yield records of achievement required or instigated by the adult who may be a parent, other relative or carer. Children enjoy painting, dressing up, and making models and anthropomorphising particular animals, carrying out activities similar to those that the youngster and his/her family and peers do to meet needs such as shelter and food. Through stories and drama the undertaking of a child may be revealed and this is one way of assessing early challenges and their solutions.

Outlined below, I use the 'Using the magnet' activity (referred to in Chapter 2, Case study 1) with Josh as an example of the format to use when using questions. However, we did not give the end point other than in words.

Exemplar activity title: find the magnet

You need

A variety of magnetic and non-magnetic items wrapped in paper, which could include a paper clip, an eraser, a bottle top, a plastic bottle top, a tin badge, a sweet, a pebble, cotton wool, a piece of tissue folded, a small pencil, safety pin, a coin (copper coins dated before 1972 are magnetic, those after are not), piece of Lego, a small round magnet or fridge magnet, a box or bag in which the items are to be placed.

Background

The learner needs to be familiar with the equipment and have the skills required and understanding to use it. It is not necessary to always set up before and after scenarios; some partnership investigations can have their target outcome described. It is crucial to ensure that a child has previous relevant experience or has the opportunity, in this exemplar, to have played with magnets or seen them at home. If not they need this exploratory play, or opportunities to observe phenomena, before you try to introduce them to something. If observing children every day and they have toys such as train sets with magnetic couplings and fridge magnets, they will have some experience of magnets and some of their properties even if they do not know the name.

Foundation experiences

The learner must have had experience of the attraction of magnets. Many Western children have experience of fridge magnets being attracted to a metal fridge. However, if the children have played with toys with magnets, like trains sets, which are joined together by magnetic coupling, they may not have had experience of repulsion.

If experiences are lacking, perhaps a simpler partnership experience needs to be set up. In true partnership activities there would be a second pile of identical items, the outcome, but with one wrapped item (the magnet) separate from the other items. Just using words requires the child to be able to visualise and comprehend the outcome s/he is seeking to achieve.

Words

Magnet, stocks, pushes away, attract, repel, pulls, pushes away, force, repulsion.

Cue question examples

- Do you know what a magnet is?
- How do you know?
- What do they do?
- Where have you seen them?
- How could we find which are the magnets in this collection of things in this box?
- How could we sort them?
- What would tell you a wrapped object was a magnet? What would you do?

Planning

A planning template for the stages is useful in planning emergent science experiences, including planning questions and the type to use.

Using the magnet activities as an example, a rubric such as that shown in Table 3.1 could be used; this rubric is the questioning employed and generated in science. The occasional use of such records is useful in plotting the development of a learner as well as for the use of the facilitator in reflecting on both their own practice and the child's participation as an active or otherwise learner.

NAME OF ACTIVITY Find the magnet
LOCATION OF ACTIVITY Play area
EQUIPMENT Items wrapped in opaque paper so they cannot be identified, some metallic, some not. E.g. paper clip, copper coins, safety pin, metal bottle top, a magnet, an eraser, a cork, a piece of soap, a small crayon, plastic bottle top, piece of folded paper, small pebble.
CHILD'S NAME Josh
VOCABULARY NEEDED TO BE UNDERSTOOD Magnet, stick, attract, materials, metal, pull, towards, push away
CUE QUESTIONS What is a magnet? What does it do? How do you know? Where have you seen/used magnets? How could we find which is the magnet? Remind them of the outcome. Describe it if necessary showing them with the items.
CONTINUATION CUES What can you do? How will you know an item is the magnet? What will happen if it is not? What do you think? Why do you think that? How will you know you are not testing the same things each time? How will you know when you have found the magnet?
LOOK What are you thinking? What are you going to do? (Socratic-pumping, challenge)
DO Watch the child manipulating the items, if they don't, suggest they pick two up. Ask what they think would happen (constructive challenge).
EVALUATION (Framing – question based summary) Can learner describe what s/he has done? Found out?
FURTHER CHALLENGE Can the learner sort the items into magnetic and non-magnetic? Unwrap the items, what are they? Is there a pattern of the things that are attracted and the things that are not if one of the things is the magnet? Why?
LINKS WITH LITERACY AND NUMERACY How many objects were wrapped up? How many things were magnetic? How many were not? Which set was the largest? By how many? What words describe the magnetic things? What words describe the non-magnetic items?
COMMENTS

TEACHER'S EVALUATION NOTE – QUESTIONS USED (planned or spontaneous)
Socratic
Pumping
Throwing back
Challenged further
Semantic, focusing and zooming

FRAMING
Question-Based Prelude
Question-Based Summary (Evaluation)

HIDDEN QUESTIONS (example of such statement)

Table 3.2 A Myers chart

Name of child:	Date:
Activity:	Activity area:
Equipment/resources needed:	Curriculum links (e.g. numeracy/literacy/ topic)
New words	Words child uses
Adult's cue questions	Child's questions
What happens	Child's account

Comments: (photos attached)

A simpler and quick to use chart is in Table 3.2. I refer to this as the Myers chart after the teacher who adapted my idea.

Recording the science from question to discovery

There are aspects of recording that we use in formal teaching that adults with their own children sometimes like to use. Adults working with children in preschool may also use some of these techniques to assess aspects of a learner's progress as well as for their own practice and records. There is also the ACCT approach (Robson, 2014), which is to analyse critical thinking skills. Here we consider the recording of the science investigation. Scientists have to communicate their findings otherwise no one else would know about them. For scientists this is most often done by writing. Remember, very young children don't write but they can draw and use drama to share their work. There are several papers about drama and science to which you may refer, for example, Dennis et al. (2014) who tell stories from much liked books read to the children, and McGregor (2012).

Art and sculpture/modelling are also valid aspects of recording that may be used by learners of any age. Indeed, some children can perform such activities even though they do not possess language or even because they prefer to do so.

Stages of science inquiry formalised

There is a pattern to a science inquiry starting with a child's observation and they or the adult working with them has a challenge or asks a question. The science shape sequence was devised originally to guide children through the stages in writing up a science report.

The sequence used geometric shapes which:

a)   would be familiar to learners from other toys, books and activities such as post boxes, toys, framed shapes in jigsaws;
b)   could be drawn easily; or
c)   could be cut easily from coloured gummed paper to stick on the child's book; or
d)   were available as part of sets of rubber stamps, sticky paper shapes or incorporated in stencils.

Each shape represents a stage in the logical sequence of science. They stand in place of the headings that are used in report writing: 'What I thought would happen', 'What I used', 'What I did', 'What did happen', 'What I found out'.

The sequence is as follows:

- a thin rectangle for the challenge, task or given experiment;
- an oval for a summary of the solution;
- a triangle for prediction;
- an oblong for the names of the group members and the job they will do in this work;
- a square for resources used (equipment materials);
- a circle for what was done;

- a rhombus (diamond) for the results or observations – 'what happened'. Several diamonds might be used if they are being written in;
- a semi circle – the conclusion – 'what was discovered'.

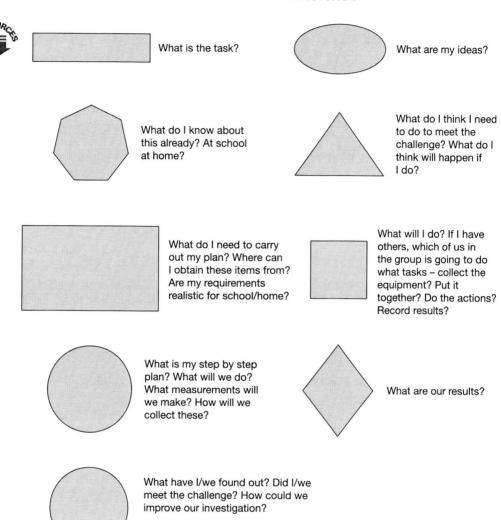

What is the task?

What are my ideas?

What do I know about this already? At school at home?

What do I think I need to do to meet the challenge? What do I think will happen if I do?

What do I need to carry out my plan? Where can I obtain these items from? Are my requirements realistic for school/home?

What will I do? If I have others, which of us in the group is going to do what tasks – collect the equipment? Put it together? Do the actions? Record results?

What is my step by step plan? What will we do? What measurements will we make? How will we collect these?

What are our results?

What have I/we found out? Did I/we meet the challenge? How could we improve our investigation?

Figure 3.1 The T-shape sequence for science

Alternative ways of using the shape sequence in science inquiry reports, which may be useful with older early learners

Wall display – class or group report

In early years education the sequence has been put on the wall and the children follow it. For making a science inquiry report an adult cuts out large shapes from display paper such as 'sugar paper' or cartridge paper onto which children contribute a word, a sentence or a drawing and this is displayed as a class report on the wall.

Hold and talk

Children may hold a shape stencil whilst they talk about that particular stage. The large stencils may be used to make card shapes for this purpose.

Follow sequence and do

Some teachers have varied this approach and put out equipment on a particular shape leaving some blank shapes in the sequence, such as the circle on which the children can put the equipment they are using whilst they 'do' the experiment.

Using the shape sequence in planning

Science and technology are about identifying a task or need, planning a strategy and trying it out, be it an experiment to investigate a question or something made to meet a need, like a litter bin.

The experimental science sequence

Interpreting the challenge or task

At the beginning, the question the children have raised, or the challenge or experiment they have been given, is received and interpreted by the learners so that they understand what is required of them. They can then put the task into their own words.

Recalling previous knowledge

Whatever knowledge and experience that the individuals have that might be relevant are contributed to a 'what we know' pool.

Forming an outline plan

The group then has to decide on the outline of an approach, a solution summary.

Designing solutions and choosing one

Once an outline approach has been discussed the designing process occurs. Various solutions may be put forward and one is selected.

Logistics – detailed planning

What equipment will be needed, where this is found, what it will do, how it will be fitted together, and in what sequence it will be used are worked through in detail. What equipment is to be used to take measurements. What is to be used for recording these? The jobs of the group are identified and agreed upon. These range from equipment collecting, equipment assembling, operator for the experiment (this may be more than one person), measurer, recorder, disassembler, reporter. The group needs to work out what the sequence of their actions will be.

Using a planning sheet with the shape sequence drawn in the margin can assist the children in planning their practical work.

The sequence of events even if modified by teacher interaction and allocation of resources or functions, can be symbolised by a sequence of shapes (based on Tunnicliffe, 1990).

Sheets with the shapes on can help learners plan, follow the task and communicate about it when completed.

Experimental notes using the sequence in 'doing'

As the inquiry is carried out it assists some learners, and especially the earliest learners, to have a sheet with the shapes on so that they can draw or write down any modifications to their original plan as the work progresses.

Teachers with younger children have found that the shapes displayed on the wall in their sequential order have assisted children in the logical progression of their work.

Some children use a sheet with the outline on upon which notes about alterations to the plan can be made.

Special needs

When planning, drawing and writing a science report the goal is achievable by taking it one step or shape at a time. In writing up a report the pupil can draw or write for one shape before being given the next shape to stamp in his/her book. The physical activity of drawing round the stencil to make the shape on paper effectively involves the children with positive results. Visually impaired learners can hold the stencils in organising and sequencing their science activities.

Variations in reporting

Children in the Foundation stage and at nursery often construct group reports on large shapes for a wall display, moving on to draw a sequence on a sheet of A4 paper. This develops into inserting a word or two as writing skills develop. This is the envisaged use of the large stencil or giving them the different shapes and seeing if they can sequence them after telling you what comes before a shoe you hold up and after, once they can recognise what a shoe stands for.

Zigzag books

These may be made from a piece of A4 (or other paper) cut in half lengthways and then folded into a concertina. Two pieces of paper may be stuck together to make a longer 'zigzag'. The shape can be drawn on one side of the fold and the drawing made on the other with the middle-sized stencil. Some children and teachers put the shape and the drawing/writing on the same page.

Flip books

These can be constructed from three sheets of A4 paper or from cutting thin exercise books in half. Taking the last page as the longest, each page is trimmed by 2 cm until the front page is the shortest page. Each piece of A4 paper is cut vertically into three strips, 10 cm wide and 21 cm long. Staple, glue or fix with wool/laces or paper fasteners the sheets, 9 in all, at the top end. Starting with the sheet next to the bottom (number 8) measure 3 cm from the bottom edge, draw a line and then cut off the 3 cm. Repeat this with each sheet until the top one, increasing the amount cut off by 2 cm each page. Thus on page 8 trim 3 cm, on page 7 trim 6 cm, on page 6 trim 9 cm, on page 7 trim 12 cm and on page 8 trim 15cm. Page 8 is the shortest page and the front one.

Big books

Learners may construct their own big books and then draw the shapes on the pages and draw the inquiry investigation within the relevant shape. If inquiring, as with Mothers Talking Everyday Science in our project at Sreepur Village in Bangladesh, learners draw what has interested them or paste in an electronic printout of a photograph they have taken of something about which they have inquired, for example, the shadow cast by a tree, a machine, a ramp that makes work easier. This technique is invaluable with learners of all ages and is language free.

Sheet with outline shapes

The shapes can be drawn on a computer and printed out. Sheets with outlines can be given to the children to write up their report inside the shapes. Many children delight in this and write, 'What we did' in circular lines within the circle. Sometimes the shapes can be cut out from thin card and made into an inquiry science mobile!

This stage is often appropriate for younger or new learners who then progress to writing their report on paper with the shape symbol in the margin or as a heading together with a written heading. The shapes assist the learners in the sequencing of their report and in sifting out the relevant facts from the irrelevant with regard to a science report for their account.

Making an inquiry science report

This shape sequence was thought up and introduced to children as an aid to assist them in the sifting and sorting of experiences and thoughts that result from a practical science activity. The reasons for writing up science are many and varied. A great many of our learners find it a daunting challenge in itself. This sequence can provide children with a logical framework within which to work. It achieves this, builds the children's confidence and is fun. Moreover, children who are not fluent in English can still follow the inquiry process and record their investigation and outcomes through drawing.

Planning and reporting engineering/design and technology

The sequence has been used successfully by primary children when designing and making solutions for a need they have identified in their work, such as the design of litter collectors. The shapes may be adapted to provide a record of which tools and materials were used in the work.

Record keeping and assessment

Assessment is a crucial part of our work if you are working in a formal situation and indeed parents and carers may be interested too.

You need to ascertain what a child already knows about something before you create a possible learning opportunity. If you know that information you can watch the progress of the learner as they explore the new situation and recognise progress in their ideas and understanding, which may or may not fit with the accepted science and be an alternative, sometimes called misconception, when compared with the accepted science. However, by mapping the progression of skills mastered and ideas developed you are assessing the learner. This recording is very important in formal learning situations and there is a need for record keeping. Using Phyllis Katz's (2012) photo journal technique and talking later with the learner about what they were doing when the photograph was taken and how their ideas and skills have changed is a very useful means of assessment as well as recording, particularly for families.

Teachers may find that using the shape sequence in their own ongoing class records of assessments of individuals for investigating and exploration attainment provides a quick framework. The shapes drawn on paper with the words of the stages (e.g. for 'jobs' there would be a number of oblongs each with a different name such as collector, operator), provide a record sheet for a pupil to keep of what they themselves have been doing. They can easily see by looking at the ticks or colour block opposite a stage in the science and technology planning whether they are being involved over a period of time in all aspects of the work. This can be used together, instead of or in turn with the question analysis record.

A progress chart such as the one below can be useful for keeping notes on the achievement a learner.

Table 3.3 Progress and achievement

Name of child:	Date:
Activity:	Activity area:
Equipment/resources needed:	Curriculum links (e.g. numeracy/literacy/topic)
Assumed previous knowledge	Skills expected to be acquired Appropriate skills they knew and used

(continued)

Table 3.3 (continued)

Vocabulary for activity	Vocabulary child used	Test questions from teacher	Child's responses	Child's questions	Child's summary of what the activity is about

Comment: e.g. learner's approach, new skills mastered, skills used.

Assessment comment and next steps:

Talking

Through talking with the learner you can assess their level of understanding, manipulative and social skills, as well as their problem-solving abilities. You can use the planning template or modify it to record what happens and assess the progress of the learner. Such a record feeds into progression. For example:

Table 3.4 Skills and practices record

NAME OF ACTIVITY
LOCATION OF ACTIVITY
EQUIPMENT
WHICH CHILD
VOCABULARY NEEDED TO BE UNDERSTOOD
VOCABULARY MASTERED
CUE QUESTIONS (pumping, throw back, challenge)
CONTINUATION CUES
LOOK (pumping, challenge)
HIDDEN QUESTIONS (example of such statement)
OBSERVATIONS?
EVALUATION (summary questions)
FURTHER CHALLENGE
LINKS WITH LITERACY AND NUMERACY
COMMENTS

Using stories

Some adults use stories to introduce a science phenomenon, which may lead to children asking questions and designing an investigation (Gatt and Theuma, 2012; Johnson, 2013). Alternatively, stories can be read and talked about once an activity has been carried out and the outcomes in the story, such as the traditional fairy story of the giant and the magical beans in Jack and the Beanstalk, or the caterpillar eating cupcakes (Carle, 2002).

If you wish to prompt a child in a certain topic it is essential that they have experience of the science principle that is being discussed.

John et al. (2013) describe how early years children in Wales used an anthropomorphic story about three baby owls after which the children drew, painted, made models and learnt about real owls.

Drama

Not all children respond to writing or even drawings. Very young children often act out something they have seen. For example, seeing dinosaur animatronics intrigued my eldest son and when we arrived home he was discovered under a pile of cushions and then emerged as we walked into the room and announced that he was a baby dinosaur emerging from its egg! (He had been intrigued by the museum exhibit of a reconstruction of a nest with eggs and a young dinosaur hatching.)

The use of drama in expressing science ideas visually and assessing the understanding of an idea is becoming more frequently used (McGregor, 2012; Dennis et al., 2014) .

General assessment

As you work with a child you are continually assessing them. Although this book is concerned with problem solving and inquiry-based science, the general demeanour of the learner will be apparent by observing the facial expression of the child, their general posture and approach to the challenge. When you are observing you may consider:

- Are they enthusiastic?
- Do they try/do they focus on the task?
- Do they talk spontaneously?
- Do they communicate with you openly?
- Do they suggest ideas and approaches?
- Do they suggest and choose items to use in their challenge solution?
- Have they the required manipulative skills to use items correctly?
- Do they grasp words and skills with interest?
- Do they apply earlier learning?
- Can you recognise their earlier experiences in the present sent work (prior knowledge)?
- Can they cooperate if working with another child?
- Do they enjoy the work or are they reluctant participants?

Such a record can be of great use to other staff, support staff and external agencies, such as the school's educational psychologist.

It is useful to compile a recording sheet, which can be dated with a particular recording of the aspect of learning in action and then filled to track progression and achievement.

Photo journals

Taking photographs of the child in action can be a useful means of recording progress. Photo journals (Katz, 2012) are becoming increasingly popular, as are photographs for the learning portfolio of the child.

Table 3.5 Achievement record

Category	Date Comment	Date Comment	Date Comment	Date Comment	Date Comment
Are they enthusiastic?					
Do they try/do they focus on the task?					
Do they talk spontaneously?					
Do they communicate with you openly?					
Do they suggest ideas and approaches?					
Do they suggest and choose items to use in their challenge solution?					
Have they the required manipulative skills to use items correctly?					
Do they grasp words and skills with interest?					
Do they apply earlier learning?					
Can you recognise their earlier experiences in the present sent work (prior knowledge)?					
Can they cooperate if working with another child? Or you?					
Do they enjoy their task?					

Field notes

The record sheet suggested earlier can be used to score the attainment of the child generally or numerically on a score scale devised by you and colleagues, say 1 for minimal interaction rising to 4 for confidently tackling the challenge.

The reflective teacher

Our job as educators and as parents is to look at the responses of our learners to experiences we have structured for them as well as their spontaneous reaction to phenomena in their environment. This requires us to reflect on the situation, in other words being a reflective practitioner. Such a process is a key aspect of our work, particularly in the early years where we are assisting a child form their foundation understanding, which will underpin subsequent and lifelong learning. Hallet (2012) discusses these vital aspects of educational practice.

Summary

Some adults working with early learners, parents, nursery staff or early years' teachers, may wish to help their learner establish the sequence of the inquiry science process and some ideas for strategies introducing this sequence are given in this chapter, as well as various ways for older learners to record what they do. Various suggestions for such are provided from which you may choose.

References

Carle, E. (2002) *The Very Hungry Caterpillar*. London, Puffin.

Dennis, M., Duggan, A. and McGregor, M. (2014) Evolution in action. *Primary Science*. Volume 131, Jan/Feb, 8–10.

Gatt, S. and Theuma, G. (2012) Inquiry-based learning in the early years through storytelling. *Journal of Emergent Science*. Winter, 12–18.

John, S., Cullen, R., Cole, D. and Cooper, C. (2013) Extended abstract: Developing the scientific curiosity of 3–7 year olds. *Journal of Emergent Science*. Issue 6. Winter, 36–38.

Johnson, J. (2013) The effect of two pedagogical approaches on the scientific development of predictions and hypotheses in the early years. *Journal of Emergent Science*. Issue 6. Winter, 6–12.

Katz, P. (2012) Using Photo Books to Encourage Young Children's Science Identities. *Journal of Emergent Science*. Issue 3. Spring/Summer, 22–28.

Hallet, H. (2012) *The Reflective Early Years Practitioner*. Sage, London.

McGregor, D. (2012) Dramatising science learning: Findings from a pilot study to re-invigorate elementary science pedagogy for five- to seven-year olds. *International Journal of Science Education*. 34(8), 1145–1165.

Robson, S. (2014) The analysing children's creative thinking framework: Development of an observational led approach to identifying and analysing young children's creative thinking. *British Educational Research Journal*. 40 (1), 121–14.

Tunnicliffe, S. D. (1990) *Challenge Science – Living Things Pupil Material and Teachers Book*. Oxford, Basil Blackwell.

Chapter 4

Foundation skills: shape, space and measure

Background: rationale for shape, space and measure

In growing from a newborn baby to a functional adult we acquire a number of skills through maturing and we learn those that are associated with our culture at which we become proficient as we age. Young children acquire understanding of aspects of mathematics, basically shape, space, number and measurement, science examples in the everyday world. Young children also gradually acquire relevant skills. Our job as educators, be it with family or school, is to assist the learners in this acquisition. Skills and understanding need be developed from the early years. Children need to be able to say why a shape is a member of the group named and recognise the names of the basic shapes and measures and be able to say them. They gradually learn the need for standard measures and how to use simple values. They progressively develop from basic ability, gradually to fine motor skills and recognition of the shapes encountered, the concepts of measurement (time, space, volume and mass – weight), and an awareness and recognition of spatial distribution of organisms and objects. These are foundation experiences essential for inquiry science.

Shape, space and measure

Learning about shape, space and measurement is fundamental mathematics. However, an understanding of these basic mathematical ideas is essential for studying science. Shapes have two forms. They are 2D (plane shapes) formed by straight or curved continuous lines; these have sides and breadth but no depth. There are 3D shapes such as spheres, cubes, cylinders (prisms) and cones.

Children must know about different kinds of shapes. For example, flat, straight-sided shapes are called polygons. Each shape has discreet attributes that belong to its special category, like a square, but also shares attributes that categorise it in a superordinate category.

- A triangle is a flat shape but with three straight lines as its sides.
- A rectangle is a four-sided polygon.
- A square is a special instance of a four-sided polygon.
- A rhombus is a special instance of a four-sided polygon.
- A parallelogram is a four-sided polygon with two sets of sides, each set parallel to the other and are the same length.

Plane (2-dimensional shapes with straight sides)

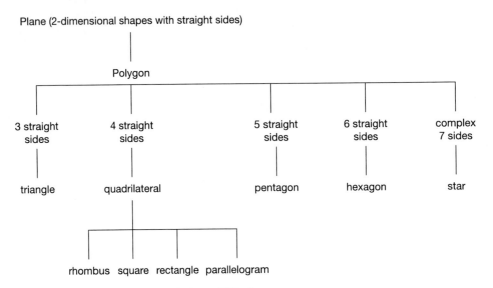

Figure 4.1 A categorisation of plane (2D) shapes

- A pentagon is a five-sided polygon.
- A hexagon has six sides.

For example, a square has four straight sides, all of the same length and the angle between the two sides at any corner is the same. A rectangle is similar but each set of two sides is the same length but the two sets of sides are not, hence the rectangle is an elongated square whereas a parallelogram does not have the right-angled angles. A rhombus has four sides, like a diamond shape, where opposite sides are parallel angles opposite each other that are equal but these pairs of angles are not the same as in a square. These are all types of square. Penta means five and hex means six, hence pentagons and hexagons.

Curved shapes

A circle is made of a curved continuous line, which is always the same distance from the centre all the way round the edge.

An ellipse is an oval or egg-shaped shape with a continuous curved line.

3D shapes

These 3D shapes have volume; this may be solid or may be a volume of air, such as a pyramid, a cuboid, or a cylinder.

A cone is a solid (3D) object that has a circular base and one corner (apex) at the narrow end.

A pyramid is a sold triangle with five sides and hence corners.

Straight sides

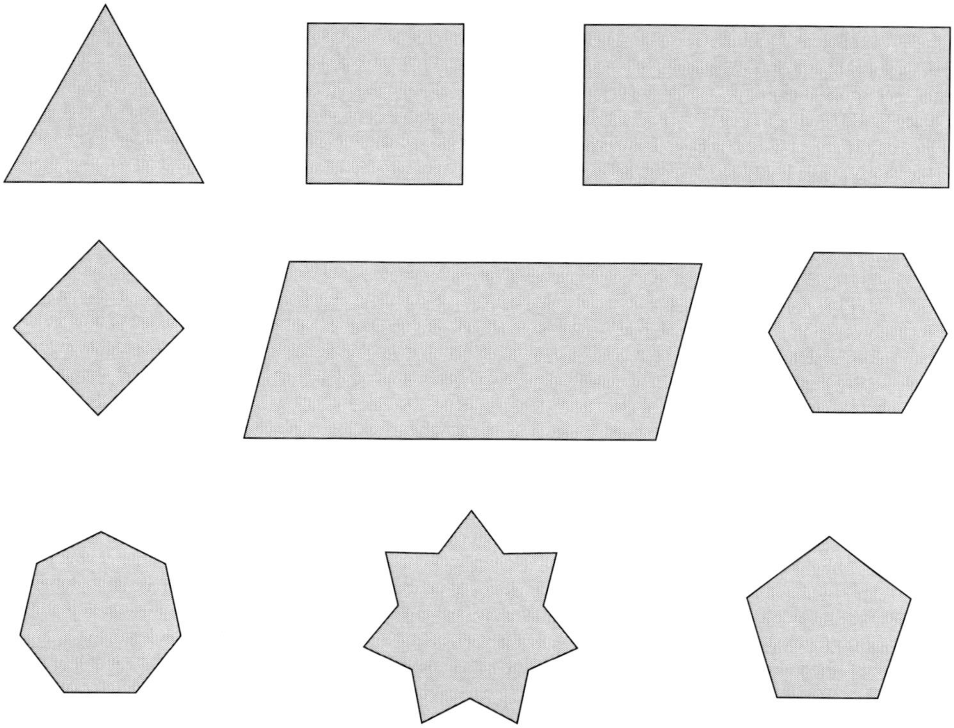

Curved sides

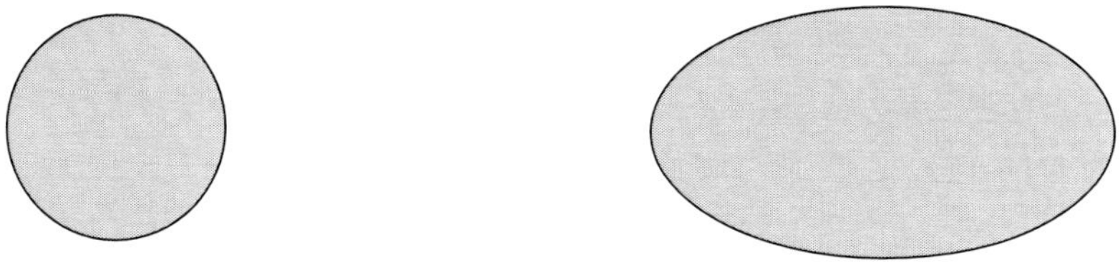

Figure 4.2 Basic Geometric 2D shapes

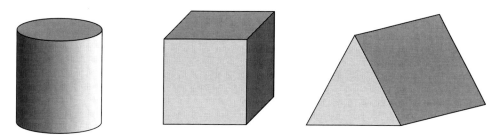

Figure 4.3 3D geometric shapes

Figure 4.4 Everyday shapes

A cuboid is box-shaped object. It has six flat sides and all angles are the same shape as a right angle. All of its faces are rectangles.

A cube is a 3D square with all sides the same length and height.

Other 3D flat-sided square shapes are called cuboids, like small cereal packages, for example. A cylinder or tube has one curved side, which has no edge. If the cylinder is stood upright the bottom or base is the same size and shape as the top, both of which are flat.

The cylinder and cuboid are also members of the group of shapes called prisms. They have the same cross-section along a length.

A cube is a box-shaped solid object that has six identical square faces.

A cylinder is a solid object with:

• two identical flat ends that are circular or elliptical;
• and one curved side.

It has the same cross-section from one end to the other.

A sphere is a 3D object shaped like a ball. Every point on the surface is the same distance from the centre.

Vocabulary

Rhombus; circle; square; sphere; cube; pyramid.

Children's ideas

Sausages

I was watching a 4-year-old girl work in the early years' kitchen area, complete with wooden replica stove, fridge, cupboard for utensils, such as a rolling pin, board, biscuit cutters and a collection of cooking items, such as baking trays and saucepans. Her ingredient was salmon pink modelling clay, which she kneaded and pummelled then split into small bits. Each one she rolled carefully and placed on the baking tray she had positioned by her board. She carefully placed the baking tray, filled with rows of pink clay 'sausages' in the 'oven' and removed it after a few minutes and announced about the sausages (for that is evidently what they were representing), "We're done. Would you like one?"

Now, whilst we can criticise this role play being acted out and point out that is not how sausages are actually made and that sausages take longer to cook than a few minutes, this young learner was not only showing creativity but a basic understanding of quantity. Although not equal in size they were in the same category of size, only varying a little in width and length. She showed how a large amount could be split into smaller units. This was the beginning of measurement.

I did point out that the 'sausages' were not all the same size. She replied, "Yes, that's not fair but that's how they are!"

Ice cream cones

When working with Josh on 3D shapes, we made a cone from a piece of paper, which wasn't in fact a square. When we had folded the paper into a 3D shape, he immediately said 'Ice cream cone', and acted out licking an ice cream.

Foundation skills

Before tackling the 'Shape, space and measure' activities children must be able to hold a pencil, draw simple shapes freehand and draw around solid 2D shapes, be able to fold pieces of paper, know the names of colours and be able to say what colour a shape is, and be able to pick up shapes and other pieces of equipment. They must know about lines, be able to point to straight lines and curved lines and be able to draw one freehand. They need an understanding that 3D shapes exist, e.g. an ice cream cone, a ball, and that such 3D shapes can be solid or hollow; they have a space. Early inquirers should be able to measure in non-standard and then standard units of length, volume and mass. They need to understand the ideas of hot and cold and have seen thermometers.

Fair testing in inquiry science

Children are very quick to talk about 'fair' and 'not fair'; such an understanding can help them understand aspects of inquiry science. However, inquiry is not only about fair testing. It is about observing something living, such as a tree, or other natural phenomena, like soil or weather. Something constructed should be included, such as a cardboard box placed outside. This could be observed over time, identifying and classifying objects, event, and organisms, seeking patterns in such observations and finding out through asking, looking it up using the Internet, and of course fair testing (Turner, 2012).

Aims of activities

Through following these activities the learners should:

- develop a basic understanding of different shapes, 2- and 3D;
- the need for measuring and fair testing in measuring, of length, volume, weight and time;
- the main units and their names used in maths and science;
- the basic instruments used – rulers, tapes, measures, scales, heat strips;
- problem solving.

Activities – shapes, space and measure

The key element of the following activities, which is also essential in their maths learning, is for the learner to be given a challenge in a question to which they answer through looking, thinking and doing. This way they generate their solution. The learners may need some prompting in different forms of questions and may need some relevant foundation pre-experiences, such as being able to fold paper or model play dough, before they start. The expertise of their adult will determine what foundation experiences are required.

Activity shapes

You need

A variety of 2D geometric shapes, cards cut out into the shapes. Coloured shapes, tape, modelling clay, pictures of shapes in everyday life, such as traffic cones, a musical instrument, triangles and square tiles, handkerchief, tissue scarf folded into triangle shape, ball, round objects, chalk, ice cream cone, tubes, modelling board, plastic knives, biscuit cutters, greaseproof paper, die, small boxes, paper and scissors. Squared paper, small bottles, masses to weigh, scales, cups or containers and measuring jugs. Water, spoons of different capacity. Or measuring spoon sets. Kitchen towel, waterproof coverings for surfaces, timer, egg timer, stopwatch, digital clock, analogue clock, calendars, rubber stamps of shapes, bathroom scales. Photographs of everyday items to show different shapes. Pictures of flowers and rest of plant (roots, stem, leaves), pictures or real leaves of differing shapes. Toy animals, e.g. farm animals or pictures of wild animals (to identify component shapes). Teddy bear or other soft toy animals.

Shapes

Should children recognise shapes, learn the names of them or the shape attributes first of all? What do you think? One day they will have to recognise shoes and be able to name them. Words such as triangle, square, rectangle, rhombus, parallelogram, oblong, hexagon, pentagon, circle, oval and semicircle, are basic to mathematics, science, design and technology and everyday encounters.

Do you teach the vocabulary or introduce the learner to a variety of shapes first and encourage them to describe them, identify such shapes in their everyday world and then introduce the name? It is up to you.

Feeling 2D shapes

Let the children play with shapes such as the brightly coloured plastic maths shapes. Try to have the same shape in different sizes and colours if possible. You can make such shapes using coloured card and laminate them, if they cannot be purchased.

Spread the shapes out on a table top. Ask each child in your group to answer one by one (if possible).

My best shape!

Which shape does the learner like the most? Why?

Ask the individual to choose their 'best shape' and say what it is that they like. It may be the colour. If so, show them the same shape but in a different colour. Do they like that one too? Why? Lead them into describing the shape. Is it because it has straight sides, feels nice to hold and stroke? Do they like the small one better than the large one or vice versa? Why?

Cutting shapes

Roll, or let the learner roll out on a board a thin piece of modelling clay (2D shapes should have no depth). Use biscuit cutters to let the children choose one shape they would like to cut from modelling clay. Choose geometric shapes. Ask for the shape name.

Recognising shapes

Have a set of shapes that you can hold and as many sets of identical shapes as you have children working with you. Tackling this is best done on a one-to-one basis.

Hold up a shape, e.g. square, and ask, "Can you match my shape by choosing it from your set? Show me by holding it up?" If their shape is put on top of your shape, do they match?

Name the shape!

Say the words of the shapes you have as 2D representations: circle, square, rectangle, triangle, oval, rhombus.

Ask: "Do you know the name of this shape?"

Hold up one. If they do name it, repeat the name and ask the child to repeat the name.

Ask: "Can you describe the shape?" They may need to be provided with a few cue words to start with, such as colour, side or big.

Repeat until all your shapes have been named.

Inside shape walks

Change location

If you are able, take the group of shape seekers out of the area and walk around the school with their 'busy' shape to see if its shape can be identified anywhere else inside the school.

Can they remember seeing any shapes in school, in the hall for instance? Some centres and homes have round stools, or round plates, round beakers, rectangular lunch boxes, a round clock on the wall, a rectangular letter box, and doors, square boxes, round door knobs or oblong benches for games or the seat of a garden bench.

The children can create a poster of shapes in school and draw the shape and the object in the room where it is seen or they could photograph the item and then draw their shape.

Children could take digital photographs of the location of their 'circle'. The children could show how the shape they have identified matched the basic shape about which they have learnt and say why.

Outside shape walk

If you have the facilities and clement weather take the shape learners outside and walk around the outside of the school. Look out for round drain pipes in older schools, gutters, rectangular bricks and manhole covers. Paving stones are commonly seen examples.

Repeat the drawings or dialogue, recording the shapes seen and identified by the learner.

Name this shape

Once back inside ask the shape learners if they know the names of any of the other shapes. What is their favourite shape called? If they do not know ask them to describe their shape. Does it have corners or no corners? Sides or no sides?

Fitting shapes together – tessellations

Can the shapes of one kind fit together like a tessellation with no gaps between them? Ask: "Can the shape fit precisely next to any part of any other shapes?" Give the names. Hold up each shape, the largest you have, and say its name. Ask: "Can you say the name too?"

Ensure the children know the words, corner, side, point, and can count up to the number eight.

Count the sides of the shapes. Arrange them in order from those shapes with the most sides, hexagon, then pentagon, then square, rectangle, oblong, parallelogram, triangle, semicircle, circle and oval.

Ask: "Which shapes do you want to see if they fit? What do you think?"

Ask, whilst holding up a triangle and square: "Will these shapes fit together with no gap between them?"

Ask: "Tell me what it looks like. How many sides?"

Ask: "Which shapes only fit together with a gap?"

Stamping patterns

If you have sets of rubber stamps and ink pads, or stickers in different geometric shapes challenge the learners to choose three shapes, e.g. star, circle and square, and make a pattern on a piece of plain paper. Each shape must touch another shape, or ask them to make the rules for fitting the shapes together.

Shape sounds

When the children can recognise the shapes, ask them which shape word they like to say the most? Par-a-llel-o-gram, rhom-bus, hex-a-gon, ob-long cir-cle, tri-ang-le, for instance are satisfying words to say. Perhaps you can compose a poem or chant with the words 2D, 3D, solid, space, volume.

Assessment!

Hold up a shape and ask for hands up for its name.

Where are the shapes?

Once the children can recognise the shapes, challenge them to go round their learning area carrying their 'best' shape and see if together they can find objects or pieces of furniture that have the same shape. If they cannot find the shape, can they think why not? Challenge your learners to think of a place in school or home where there is a piece of furniture that does have a shape that they recognise.

Encourage them to repeat it with another shape.

It's quiz time!

Have a quiz, by arranging 2D shapes on a table in front of you but with a screen. Get children or a child to carry out this useful activity, one-to-one and hold up a shape and ask them to match it and name the shape.

Ask: "Why is this shape a xxxx?" "What makes this a special type of shape?" A rhombus, for example, is a parallelogram with two sides the same length, unlike a square with four equal sides. Nor are there right angles in it. Ask the children to match similar shapes (e.g. with four straight sides) with the same shape.

Assessment records

You can fill in a chart for assessment purposes of each child. First, choice of shape, and where they found the shape in the room (if they did). Repeat the shape quiz (see above) at the end of the work as the summative assessment.

Assessment

Ask them to keep a score of how many they know. You can record this for assessment. Take a photograph of the children conducting this task.

Inquiry questions

Make a note of questions you used with the child and their questions too.

Space

3D shapes have volume and they take up space.

Cones

Provide the learner with a square piece of paper and ask them to make a cone.

Is there any shape they can make with the piece of paper? Triangles are often suggested. Step-by-step instructions can be found on the web, e.g. http://snapguide. com/guides/make-a-chatterbox/.

Obtain a square piece of paper and make a chatterbox, an excellent activity in folding triangles.

Making a half square = rectangle (a polygon)

Challenge the learner to make a rectangle from a piece of squared paper.

"What do you think happens if you fold the paper in half? What shape is that?"

Body shapes – animal, human and plants

"Do we have any of the shapes such as a circle or rectangle in our bodies?"

Have an outline of a human body (or get a child to draw around the outline of another peer).

Look at the outline – are there any shapes? E.g. a head is round, legs are long rectangles, the upper arm is like a cylinder.

Show a teddy bear or other soft toy. Ask: "Has Teddy any shapes? What can you see?"

Have some pictures or animal models. Look at these; can the learner find any shapes in these? The torso is like a rectangle. What shape does a head look like in the picture? Do different animals have different shaped heads?

Plants

Have some pictures of plants and flowering plants. "Are any flowers star shapes, or circular? What shape are the leaves? What shape are the fruits (e.g. tomatoes, orange, cucumber, cabbage)?"

3D solids

Vocabulary

Ball, spheres (a marble for example), semicircle, quarter circle, half, triangular, cone, cylinder.

You need

Modelling clay, paper, a ball, a plastic or blunt metal knife and a cutting board, biscuit cutters, square and cuboid biscuit cutters, 3D shapes, mathematical ones and everyday, cylinders e.g. yoghurt drinks, hollow, small piece of pipe, boxes such as triangular chocolate box, tissue boxes, rectangular and square (cuboid) protractor to show semicircle shape, ice cream cone and picture of traffic cone, oranges, apples, cabbage, cucumber, a hardboiled egg.

Activities

Fruit shapes

What shape is an orange? A tomato, a cucumber and egg? Have some modelling clay on the table.

Ask the child, "Can you make a ball with the modelling clay? (Sphere, a 3D circle.)

What shape is the ball? Has it a shape? What happens if you cut the ball down the middle?"

Lay the two halves on the table, flat side up.

Ask: "What shape is the flat surface of the cut through the ball?"

Semicircles

Ask: "What happens if you cut one of these half circles in half?"

Fractions

Ask the learner to describe what is seen. What name do they think this shape could have (a half or semi circle)? How much of the circle is left?

The result is a quarter circle. If this is cut again the pieces are eighths.

Ask the learner how many eighths there are in a ball shape (four quarters and each quarter halved). How can they find out?

Make a small sphere. Ask the child what they will find if they cut the circle through from one side to another, but at a slant. When they have achieved this, ask them what shape the flat surface is.

Rectangles and squares in 3D

Squares are more difficult to make out of modelling clay. It is difficult to get the sides flat. Using flat plastic or wooden pieces can be one way of obtaining flat sides or putting the modelling clay in a small plastic box out of which you can tip the shape if it does not stick. Try lining the box with tracing paper or something similar.

The easiest method is to mould the square or rectangle by hand. The result is approximately a square. Alternatively, square and cuboid biscuit cutters are available.

Ask: "What is special about the sides of a 3D square? Does your 3D square show these?"

Tubes – cylinders

Obtain some cardboard tubes such as from kitchen towel. Ask: "What shape is this? From the side?"

"What shape is this kind of tube? What shape is it looking at the ends? What happens if you cut a tube long ways?"

Ask the child if they have ever seen a shape like this around school, home or the streets.

Ask: "What happens if you cut across the tube?"

Cube making

Make a cube from paper.

You need a square piece of paper, clear adhesive tape, scissors, a ruler, and a pencil. Challenge the learner to see if they can work out what needs to be done. There are several YouTube clips and other websites that give step-by-step instructions demonstrating how to fold paper to make a cube.

Find the cuboid

Have an assortment of boxes including square tissue boxes, wooden bricks, and Lego bricks. Ask children to find the square. Can they find the cuboids?

Prisms

Have some tubes and a triangular chocolate box if possible; here we have prisms with different flat ends and cross-sectional shapes.

Cut out 3D shapes

You need special biscuit cutters, but if they are not available you can cut out squares, cuboids shapes and some 3D shapes. Challenge the learner, "What is different about the 3D shapes from the 2D shape you have cut out?" (thickness).

Cones

Hollow cone

Provide a new piece of paper that is square. Challenge the learner, "Can you can make a cone?" Cue the challenge: "Like an upside down ice cream cornet." Provide some sticky tape or glue to fix the joins when the construction is deemed done.

Ask: "Can the cone stand up? What happens if you try with the pointed end? What happens if you try with the other end?"

Ask the learner to examine their cone. Ask: "What shape is the outline?" Turn the cone upside down so that the pointed end is facing downwards. Ask: "What is the shape?"

3D solid cone

Making a 3D cone with modelling clay is tricky. Can the learner try? What does s/he need to do to the clay to build a cone?

3D walks

Challenge: "Are there any 3D shapes in our room/in the classroom?" Look out for round pipes, lampshades, pencil sharpeners, erasers, the base of a wastepaper bin, round pencils and crayons, wheels on toys, a wall clock, door knob, seat of a stool.

School 3D shapes

Walk down the corridor, walk around the school, are there any 3D shapes? Ask: "Are there any other round shapes outside the classroom but inside school?"

Outside shapes in 3D

Walk and look at the outside of school. Ask: "Are there any three-dimensional shapes?"

Look out for round (cylindrical) drainpipes, semicircle cross-section gutters, footballs, climbing frames with squares and rectangles, round hoops for games, cones.

Assessment

Make a plan of the classroom on the white board (or iPad or laptop). Ask the children with whom you are working, "Can you mark on the plan places where you can find four different shapes?"

(A 2D bird's eye view of the classroom if they can interpret such, or draw a perspective of the classroom inserting the major pieces of furniture etc.)

See how many shapes they can recall.

You could repeat this activity for a school corridor and outside of the school, a wall and the grounds or playground. Sometimes drawings and copying one piece of paper is easier, especially when working with only one child. If you have iPads you could have a photograph of the classroom, the inside of the school, the outside of the school. Ask the child to point out the shape of their choice on the photographs. Printing their photographs of something a certain shape, such as a square, a circle, in the room or outside, is another option for this assessment exercise.

Was there inquiry? Fill in the relevant record chart.

Position

Space is often understood as position of objects. It is important for inquiry science that children can describe the position of a body part, a flower at the side of a stem, a flower at the top of a stem, or the location of organisms in relation to their surroundings by using position language.

Vocabulary

Above, below, beside, next to, side, top, bottom, behind, under, besides.

My body parts position

Challenge the learner, "Can you put one hand above your head? Behind your back? Under your knee? Next to your other hand?" This activity checks to assess their understanding of the positional words used.

Have some models, e.g. a village with people. Ask the children to place a named Lego person next to a door or a tree. It depends on what scenario you have with movable parts but use the words to check that the children understand what the word means and can position parts according to your instruction. Ask them to explain the positional name of where the item has been placed.

Measurement

A measurement is a methodical way to give a number to each item that needs to be measured so that you can talk about the item with meaning, compare it with another, like the size of clothes, distance to space, weight of something. In everyday meaning, a measure is about finding the length, area, and volume of items and being able to compare them with a standard; it's rather like a fair test, each new measurement of an item can be compared against the control, which remains the same. So a standard measure for a particular dimension is referred to in order to make a fair comparison. The learner needs to be able to count up to at least five.

> **Words to use**
>
> Compare, long, wide, tall, short, weigh, measure, volume, standard, same, bigger than, smaller than, the same size as, longer, shorter, equal, heavier, lighter, less heavy, less long, weight, mass, metre, centimetre, volumes, capacity, amount, measure, jug, cup, beaker, syringe, spoon, plate, gram, kilogram.

Why do we measure?

We need to measure so we can match things to compare them using the same unit of measurement, e.g. in building a box or making a cake. We need a value of the measurement so that we can compare one measurement of a similar item with another measurement of different-sized items of the same kind, e.g. amount of water a mug holds.

This sequence of activities and dialogue seeks to establish the need for measurement, use of non-standard and then standard measures and introduce learners to the standard measurements, millilitre, litres, centimetre, metre, second, minute, hour, gram, kilogram.

Weighing

Josh, when four years old, was fascinated by the bathroom scales. When he stood on them the needle moved. When he tried his soft toy on the scales the needle did not move as far. He was fascinated. This was an early experience of measuring weight (mass) and learning that different objects have different values.

Half a biscuit

Alan as a toddler was shouting from his cot; his father went to see what was the cause of the noise. Alan announced he wanted another biscuit. "No", his father said, "you've had your supper and your biscuit". "No", said Alan. "Biscuit". After a silence, his father said, "much?" Alan replied, "Half". The deal was struck; the child had an understanding of whole and half.

Me and you

Ask the learner, "How big are you? Are you as big as I am?"

Continue with a measurement and the dialogue. Are they bigger, or smaller? Ask them in what directions are they 'measuring' you – height and width? Heaviness (mass)? What do they say?

Them and other things

Ask the learner about themselves in relation to other objects. Are they taller than the top of the back of their chair? Are they wider than their chair? Are they taller than the seat height of an adult chair? What is the difference between the measurement and their own chair? How can they show you? What else could they do to compare the heights?

So what is big?

What do they mean by 'big'? What is big? Is it all of them upwards, across, round or just a part of them? How do they know whatever they mention is big, bigger, or thin?

Ask the learner if they ever measure anything or watch anyone else measure something?

For instance, how much water they put in a mug or how much fuel (petrol) someone puts in a car. Which size bottle of juice is bought?

Have pieces of paper (squared) and pieces of string, wool or ribbon, each of varying lengths, e.g. 5 cm, 10 cm, 15 cm, 20 cm, 30 cm. Have the same lengths of both materials. Ask them to look at their fingers; can they measure the longest finger? Does it match the length of the string? Is a piece of string too short or too long? How can you explain to someone how long your finger is? What do you really need in order to talk about measurement?

Have a collection of measuring items on the table, e.g. measuring jug, scoop, spoon, medicine syringe, scales for food, bathroom scales, ruler, tape measure, height chart.

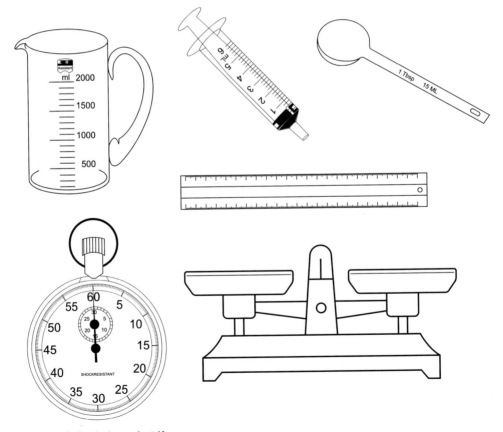

Figure 4.5 Find the cuboid?

What are these?

Encourage the child to look at and touch the items. Do they make any comments about them? If not or you want to amplify their dialogue, ask some questions. Ask: "Have you ever seen any of these before? Where? Who was using them? Where? What were they doing? What was being measured?"

Scenario

Make up a scenario about measurement; suggest perhaps that someone has given you a pair of shoes but you don't know for whom they are meant. Ask if any of you, or the child with whom you are working and you, could just as easily wear the shoes? What did the learner think? What about baby bootees? Could one of you wear them?

You could have a pair of disposable slippers or some other footwear or other items to show them.

What about a hat, would it fit both of you just as well? Or a dress or shirt? Or gloves? If you have adult objects that can be tried on by a child, ask them to test their idea if they say you could both fit whatever is in discussion.

Ask them why. Ask them if they think the item would be too big for them or too small for the adult, and why?

Length

Show the learner some items of the same object but of differing sizes, e.g. Lego figures, dolls, teddy bears, toy cars, building bricks and Lego bricks.

Let the learner look at and handle the objects. What do they do? What do they say? Ask in short question form the following sequence, when they have orientated themselves to the objects:

Which is the biggest?
Biggest in what way? Which is the longest?
Longest in what way? Which is the shortest?
Shortest in what way? How can you tell?
Can you measure them? How?

Ensure they or you touch each object when they talk about it, so you know which one they are talking about.

Roll a ball

Have a selection of balls, particularly two small ones, such as a tennis ball, and a larger one, such as a football. Challenge: "I wonder if the same balls roll the same distance as each other? How can we find out?" Ask the learner to choose a ball. "What will you do? Why?" Then choose a ball and repeat the activity, this time rolling the new ball along the same surface.

Ask them to predict, "What happens if . . . . . .? . . . which ball rolls furthest? How far? How much further?" How can you tell how far the balls have rolled?

What does the learner suggest for measuring the distance? Do they suggest standard or non-standard measures such as their foot lengths? How do you measure the distance that your ball travelled? Use a standard measure. Talk about your result and their result.

Fair test

Ask: "Was the test fair? What wasn't fair?"

With two different people rolling the ball, they each might have rolled it at a different strength. How could the test be made fairer? If the learner has trouble thinking about it being fair, ask, "Were both balls rolled from the same starting point? . . . on the same type of surface? By the same person therefore the same push?"

One roller!

Follow what the learner suggests. Do they think the balls will roll away the same distance if the same person rolls them? Why? Ask: "What happens if the balls are the same, rolled by the same person? Different balls? What happens if each ball is rolled on a different surface?" Ask: "What do you think will happen? Why? How can you make a fair measurement of the distances so you can compare?"

What does the learner suggest?

Compare the distance – a fair measure

To make it a fair measurement what do you need to do?

Have different lengths of wool or string or strips of squared paper and a marker to mark the end of the distance. See how many small strips are needed to measure the distance. How many small strips are there in one long strip? Introduce a 30 cm ruler and a metre rule. Show them the distances rolled by each ball measuring it for each roll using the strips of cm squared paper (or another measure).

Volume

Have a row of differing sized mugs, plastic cups or jugs, for example. You need a source of water, a large measuring jug with a scale, some empty measuring jugs, a waterproof sheet to protect the work surface and absorbent cloths to wipe up any spills.

Ask the children what the objects are you have set in a row. What are they for? What goes inside them? Do they all contain the same amount of water when they are full? How will they decide what is full?

How can they find out if there is the same volume of water in each container? How can they measure?

A spoonful of medicine

Have some medicine syringes, a 5 ml measuring spoon and a beaker of water (more fun if it has some food colouring, e.g. pretend it is green medicine for Teddy). They should have their plastic cups each with a mark for 25 ml on (5 times the volume of a full syringe or spoon). Ask: "Have you seen these before? Where, if so? What are they used for?"

Talk about taking medicines and pills. Ask them, "Why is it important to know the amount of medicine that is being given in a dose?" Invite them to talk about the items. Ask: "Have you ever used these items?"

Water jug

Have some water in a jug or dry sand to be measured. Encourage them to find out how to fill them by using the syringe and spoon. Have two empty pots, small see-through beakers or foil cake holders or same-sized egg cups for them to empty their syringe or spoon into. How many syringefuls does it take to fill a plastic beaker to the mark?

How many spoonfuls of water does it take to fill another beaker with a mark in the same place?

What can a child say about the volume of the syringe and spoon? Ask: "Do these two measuring items measure the same volume? How could you find out?"

What do they find out from their inquiry? How can they tell someone else what they found out?

Scoops and spoons

Have a set of scoops usually used for measuring powder in cooking or serving spoons. Have some powder, e.g. flour (and protective covering for work surfaces). Ask the children, "Which scoop is the largest? The smallest?"

Continue the dialogue: Which will measure the biggest volume of powder? Why do they think that? Which do they think is the smallest? How can they make sure their prediction is correct? What will they do?

Why tell people?

Prepare some empty drink cartons, cans and bottles. Show the learner where the volume in millilitres is marked on the different containers. What would happen if the amount were not marked on?

Would it be fair to the people buying the drinks if they did not know how much there was? Why do they think the amount is marked on?

Mass

We usually refer to weights of things, but correctly it's the mass. Weight depends on the pull of gravity hence spacemen appear weightless; however, their mass has not changed, the pull of gravity on them has. So, everyday weights should be called masses.

Weighing by hand

Have a selection of objects such as a polystyrene ball, a rubber ball, an orange, a potato or an onion, approximately the same size. The items can be placed in a thin polythene food bag.

Ask the children if the objects look similar. What shape are they? How can you tell if they weigh the same? What do they think? Encourage the children to pick up each item and hold it in one hand. What do they think? What happens if they compare one item with one of the others? Then the next object, then the last? What do they think? How can they keep a record of what they think?

Checking with a balance

You need scales with a linear scale or show them a beamer balance scale with buckets into which you can put the object with which you are comparing the others. What happens if the object is heavier than the one you held? What happens if the object is lighter? What happens to the side of the balance with the first object in?

How can you check their conclusion? What do you need?

I'm the heaviest ... or lightest!

> ## You need
>
> Bathroom scales in kilograms, beamer with two pans or bucket scales, objects to be weighed e.g. teddy bear, beanbag, masses (the red plastic stacking ones are useful), centicubes.

What is heavier than you? What is lighter? Am I? Is Teddy?

What is the learner's response to the challenge? "Is xxx, e.g. Teddy, heavier than you or lighter? How can you find out? Which of you weighs the most? What do they think? Why?"

How could you test their hypothesis? What do they think? Which scales will they use? Why? What do they find out?

How can you put a value on the weights? What is the difference in the weight of a child compared with something else they choose to be weighed against? Can they tell a friend what they found out? Is it easier to tell someone when you have a number to tell? What numbers are used to describe weights?

Time

The whole point of having a standard measure for time passing is that the duration of an event can be compared fairly. These activities are designed to assist learners in realising that a standard way of comparing duration is a fair understanding of days being a period of time, as are seasons and years, which is also important for learning science as well as an everyday experience.

Time for?

Show a timer such as a cooking timer; a digital and analogue clock; a stopwatch or a phone with a stopwatch. Ask: "Do you know what these things do?" Invite the child to look at and touch the timers that s/he recognises. Ask: "Do you know how any of the things (timers) work?"

Show them the stopwatch or cooking timer and discover together how it works; the learner may already know. Talk about it. Suggest you time an activity such as collecting a book. Or decide how long you can have for an activity such as walking to the classroom door.

Ask: "What do you do? What happens? How do you know the time you decided has passed?"

Time signals in clothes – in a day

Have a collection of different clothes or pictures of them, e.g. pyjamas, slippers, shoes, sweaters, trousers, jeans, football boots, plimsolls, t-shirt.

Time signals in clothes – in a year

Have a collection of mittens, swimming trunks, sun hats, swimming costume, sunglasses, flip flops/sandals, umbrella.

Seasons

Ask: "Do you do different things at different times of the year?" Cue with words like "holiday, birthday, Christmas".

Times in the day

Pose the question, "Is it time for play?" Ask the learner what times they know of in their school day.

They might say story time, circle time, and play time, home time, lunchtime. Ask how they know when it is the time for such changes in their activities. What do they say?

Do they mention numerical value? How do they know when it is time? How do adults know what the time is for doing different activities? What do people use clocks and watches for? Ask: "What do you do at night? When do you know it is night?"

What time of year is it?

How do you know? What other times of the year are there? Have some pictures of the different seasons in your country. What is different in each picture from the others? Maybe it is leaves on the trees, fruit such as apples on trees, strawberries on the plant, or very sunny days? Perhaps it is flowers blooming or perhaps trees that have leaves. At what time of year do the trees start to lose leaves or have no leaves? Do any lose their leaves? Do any keep their leaves? Or is the weather different, such as snow or very heavy rain at certain times?

What season is it?

What do you call the different times of the year? How can you tell what time of year it is? What do you do in different seasons. What do you do that is the same? What do you do that is different? Why?

Time to roll? How long does my ball roll? Is it more or less time than yours?

Devise an activity that involves comparing how long an event lasts. For example, rolling the same ball but rolled by two different people along the same route to see whose ball rolls the longest. The length of a corridor or playground is a useful distance. You need a third person, another learner perhaps, so the adult can count and time when two children are rolling.

Decide which of you will roll the ball. Have the counter, say, "Go". Let a ball roll; when it comes to a stop, have the other ball rolled. The non-roller person can count the duration of the other ball roll. Tell them to record how many counts. How many counts do each of you measure? Are they the same? Make sure each count is written down for each person.

Say person 1 rolled the ball for xx counts by xx. Repeat the rolls again with a stopwatch. You need a third person to operate the watch etc. for each time. Compare the results from the stopwatch (digital preferably) to the counts.

Are the counts the same? Or are they different? Do the counts agree with the timer results?

Car counts!

Explain that if you count one and two and three . . . .at a normal speaking rate, this is a way of counting in seconds. Try it with the activity, also timing with other timers.

Have an egg/sand timer, a digital stopwatch and a clock with a second hand. You need a toy car. Ask how long it takes for the toy car to run a certain distance. What distance will you choose? Can you go in the school hall or on the playground for a long roll? How can you measure the time? Do the different measures give the same result?

Assessment

Ask the learner how people tell the time in school and how they know what the time is for doing things. What do people use a calendar for? Why do people have clocks? Ask what sort of measuring instrument could we use? Please show me how. (Show them an egg timer and ask what it does.)

Show pictures of different times of the day or items and actions associated with times, such as a bowl of cereal, toothbrush, food on a plate, a TV, sun, moon, pyjamas. What can the learner tell you about these?

Can the learner describe how it is possible to time an event such as getting changed for swimming or outside play, putting coats on at home time?

Temperature

Words to use: hot, cold, same as, thermometer, colder than, warmer than, scale, numbers 34, 35, 36, 37, 38, 18, 19, 20, 21, 22, 23, temperature, degrees.

You need

Objects of varying temperatures, such as a container with a sealable lid, a snack-pot or a self-seal polythene sandwich bag full of ice cubes, one with some hot water, one with lukewarm water, a thermometer or a heat/fever strip.

The learner must be able to read digits or appreciate a lower and a higher number or be told so. Useful pictures could include ones of a sofa, icy snowy landscape, hot sunny landscape, desert and ice flow.

What is the weather? Hot or cold?

Show the pictures. Ask the learner, "What do you think the temperature is in each picture? Hot or cold? What makes you say that? How do you know?"

Ask: "Have you been to a cold place? How did you know it was a cold place? What was it like? How did you feel?" Ask: "Have you been to a hot place? Where? How did you know it was a hot place? What did it feel like to you? What did you want to do?" Talk about what they say.

Hot or cold?

Ask: "Do these containers feel the same to you? What do they feel like?"

"Which is the warmest?"

"Which is the coldest?"

"Why do you think they feel different?"

"Do they feel hotter or cooler than you if you touch your skin on your forearm?"

Measuring the temperature

Digital thermometers for human use will measure a narrow range around the human body temperature (about 36.5 degrees Celsius), so will fever strips. Floating bath thermometers can be put in bowls of water, not too cold or hot.

Depending on what you have arranged, have items that are warm. Fever strips/forehead strips are the best to use as they change colour when they rise or fall in temperature but the objects in which they are used need to be within the range of the temperature measures.

Perhaps you can set the room temperature? Is the thermostat digital? If it is, you can ask the learner to read the numbers. Talk about the temperature in the room. What does the outside temperature reach when it is summer? When it is winter?

Overall assessment

You can tell how the learner tackles the activities and responds to the challenges and your questions, how much they understand and have grasped. Can they explain to you the essence of what they have been doing? However, filling in a summative assessment chart, such as the ones below can help for record keeping and further planning.

Final assessment activities

Shape understanding

Hold up one of some everyday items of different shapes such as a tissue box, a book, a blown-up round balloon, a cone made from paper, a folded piece of paper in the shape of a triangle, a ball, a wire coat hanger (hide the hanging hook).

Ask: "Do you know the name of this shape?"

Ask: "Can you describe the shape?" They may need to be provided with a few cue words to start with, such as colour, side or big.

Around the room

Challenge them to find three things in the room where you are that have a different shape.

Roll a ball

Provide some modelling clay and a board, with the modelling clay in a flat piece or a lump.

Challenge them to make you a sphere. How?

Give them a square box and ask them to describe it. What is it like? Solid or not? How many sides and so on? Can they name the shape?

Space

Provide a twig with leaves. Ask the learner to describe where the leaves are positioned on the twig.

Where?

If you have shelves in the room place a well known object on one of them and ask the learner to describe where the item is – where is its position? High up, low down on the shelves, to the side but higher than them, and so on.

Measure

Give them a plastic cup and ask them to fill it half full – with water or beads or similar. Ask them how they know it is half full.

Provide several items of various sizes such as a book, a lentil, a ball, a toy car, a Lego brick, a shoe, adult and child.

Ask the child to tell you which is the biggest. Why have they chosen that? How is it bigger than X or Y? Is it longer? Deeper? Heavier?

Recording

Fill in a relevant recording chart for all the shape, space and measure activities (see Chapter 3).

Expected outcomes

After working at the suggested activities as appropriate for what you consider their aptitude, a child should be able to:

- Identify and name the commonly used geometric 2D shapes and describe their basic properties.
- Identify and describe the common 3D shapes.
- They should have increased their vocabulary and their skill of explanations as well as manipulative skills and recognised the need for standard measures, so they can compare measurements for the same object and know about length, volume, mass, time and temperature measures.
- Be aware of using fair tests when appropriate and be able to use simple measures and know the name of the main standard units.
- Be able to measure in various ways simply and understand the need for measure.

Reference

Turner, J. (2012) It's not Fair. *Primary Science*. Volume 121, Jan/Feb.

Chapter 5

Living things: ourselves

Brief background

Learners need to understand the external parts of their body, which is built on the basic vertebrate plan of a backbone, a head and four limbs. Humans walk upright, bipedally, unlike most other vertebrates, which move using their four limbs when swimming, running or flying. Humans are mammals and have hair, and sets of teeth, which are not all the same as they are in other groups, such as crocodiles, which have peg like teeth that are all the same, whereas humans have four different sorts of teeth. All animals need to find their food and so do we humans. We also have to get the food and drink into our mouths. Our eyes face forwards and our field of vision overlaps so we have stereoscopic vision but we cannot see much at the sides of us, unlike animals whose eyes are on each side of their face. We can breathe whilst we talk or even breathe, talk and eat because we have a hard roof in our mouth. Our body temperature is kept about the same, around 37 degrees Celsius, unless we get very cold or have a fever when we get hotter, as the body tries to fight off the bacteria or virus causing the fever. We, like other mammals, have a mechanism for cooling down if too hot, and have a way of trying to get warmer when cold by moving, shivering and developing goose bumps. We also control our body temperature by the clothes we wear and the places we go, which have heating or cooling.

Children's ideas

Children are fascinated by themselves and have to learn the parts of their own body and what they do. This they do in the early years. They also acquire information through hearing others talk about the external and internal body, such as the existence of organs inside their bodies. I worked with a class of 4-year-olds, who understood the existence of different internal organs; some children knew there is a stomach and some knew there are bones, and some knew of a brain and some knew that there is a heart, which is always depicted in their drawings in the iconic love heart shape. At this age they are learning what they can and cannot do with their bodies and such knowledge provides a reference point for understanding other animals, especially mammals.

This group of preschool children held this conversation with each other whilst looking at chimps in London Zoo:

GIRL: "They are doing things like us."
GIRL: "They eat and breathe."

GIRL: "They don't talk like us."

GIRL: "No, they just go pee!"

GIRL: "But they can swing on ropes and they have babies like us and they're naughty like us."

GIRL: "I'm not naughty."

GIRL: "They are funny, looks like they have four hands, we've two."

GIRL: "Look at the funny little one, he's so cute, that's a baby."

A 5-year-old girl exclaimed whilst looking at a gorilla, "Look, it's got hands like us!"

A boy remarked that the animal (gorilla), walked on two legs like him!

They interpreted what the animals were doing in terms of what they knew about themselves, eating, feeding, breathing, moving, talking, hugging, kissing, and interpreted the behaviours of the animals as naughty.

Aims of the activities

•   To ensure that the child learns the names for the major external parts of the human body.

•   To identify these parts on themselves.

To find out that:

•   All humans are built to the same patterns.

•   Humans have hair on their skin which is waterproof.

•   Humans are warm.

•   Humans walk on two legs.

•   Humans need to find their food and drink.

•   Humans have teeth.

•   Humans need to prepare some food before they eat it.

The human pattern is very similar to other animals with fur.

Words

Body, arm, leg, right, left, hand, wrist, forearm, upper arm, elbow, back, neck, head, ears, eyes, hair, skin, front, back, abdomen, chest, leg, knee, calf, thigh, foot, ankle, fingers toes, teeth, jaw, mouth, tongue, temperature, square, rectangle, circle, ellipse, moving, balance, wobble, walking, running, hopping, jumping, creeping, bottom shuffle, sliding on feet, sliding on floor, hand stands, rolling, breathing, locomotion, volume, tape measure, clothing, weather, exercise, movements, breathing, soaked, wet, hear, winter, summer, cold, hot, spring, autumn.

Foundation skills

The learner needs to be able to listen, draw and recognise the names of the shapes found in the body, a circle and rectangle are the main ones. They need to know how to use a hand lens (hold it to the eye and bring the object being looked at up to the learner's eye). They should know about waterproofing and that there is a difference between absorbing water with something, such as kitchen towel, which gets wet as the water is soaked up and water on the skin, which becomes wet but is not soaked up. They should be able to use a dropper or straw to produce a drop of water. They should be able to stand on one leg and know how to try to keep their balance! Further, they should be able to count and use simple measuring instruments, like tape measures, rulers, squared paper and rulers.

You need

Soap, water, a bowl, a white towel or kitchen towel, large piece of construction paper, felt tips, wellington boot, piece of polythene, a piece of waterproof paper, a piece of filter paper or kitchen towel (absorbent) a dropper, a beaker of water, protective covering, sponge, egg ring, bell, a tin, a triangle, drum, pencil, a small book, cup, ball, plastic knife, an eraser, a ruler, safety pin, plastic coin, pictures of different types of clothing for different times of the year, pictures of different ways of moving across a surface, dropper, straws, dish with water, sunglasses, PE/play clothes, mittens/gloves, scarf, umbrella, short socks, big coat/anorak, bobble hat, shoes, hoody, swimming trunks/bathing costume, flip flops, small mirror, sandals, trainers, woolly jumper/sweater, shorts, sun hat, goggles, summer dress, long trousers, vest, long socks, T-shirt.

Body parts!

Draw the outline of a child's body on a large piece of paper, flip chart paper or a piece of light coloured sugar or construction paper.

Shapes!

Based on the size of the children in your class, cut out rectangles for a pair of legs, which should be approximately the same size and shape of the upper and lower leg to complete a whole limb. Cut out a large rectangle to represent the torso. Cut out a circle, the size of a head. What other shapes do you think the children will recognise? If you draw ear flaps are they elliptical? Is the neck square?

Ask: "Can you look at this outline and think, what is it of? Why do you think that?" Depending on what they reply, hand them the shapes you have prepared.

Challenge: "Can you find any shapes like this in the body outline?" Ask them where they match best.

Ask: "What shape is that? Why have you put it there? What part of you is it covering? How does it fit?"

Name bits!

Write the names of the main external parts of the body that the children need to learn on sticky notes. Perhaps use these words: head, neck, ears, eyes, mouth, nose, hair, chin, cheek, chest, abdomen, back, shoulder, elbow, wrists, hand, fingers, upper leg, hip, lower leg, ankle, foot, toes, heel.

Ask the children to name a part of the human body. When they say the name give them the sticky note with that name of the body part written on and invite them to attach it to the body.

Name your part

You could have the children stick the labelled note onto the appropriate body part of themselves, if you think that a suitable task. Take photographs of the labelled body for display, children's record or portfolios.

A useful assessment opportunity

Use a similar activity at a later date as a formative assessment. Make an outline of a child and write the name of various outside parts of the body. Give your learner one Post-it or other form of label with a part of the body name on it and tell them the name and ask them to stick the label on the named part. Record if they can do this and if not what they did.

Body covering

You will need: a hand lens, a dropper or straw, a small cup of warm water, a towel (paper or cloth), small pieces of kitchen towel or filter paper, pictures of different weathers and clothing items for different weather.

Looking at skin?

Ask: "What does your skin look like? How can you find out?"

Talk about their suggestions. Show them the hand lens and ask what it does. Let them find out themselves by looking at the different items first.

Challenge: "What does your skin look like? How can you find out? Which bits are you going to look at? Why? Have you looked at the upper side of your arm? What do you see? What about the palm of your hand? Are they different to look at?"

Follow their suggestions.

Ask: "What can you see? What words describe it? Is there any equipment you can use to help look?" Show them the hand lens and check their understanding of its use.

Challenge: "Does your skin look different when you use the lens? How? Why?"

Waterproof

Challenge: "What would happen if you put a small piece of sponge in water? What is the sponge like before you put it in water? (or the kitchen towel before you put water on it?) What do you think will happen? How can you find out what does happen? What do you need to do before you answer my question?"

Cue the learner with prompts to submerge the sponge in water or drops of water on the paper towel. Water will be absorbed.

Ask: "Do all things take in water when put in it? How can we find out? What would you like to test?"

(Keep a note of what children suggest and their reasoning.)

Roll off!

Have a wellington boot, piece of polythene, a piece of waterproof paper, a piece of filter paper or kitchen towel (absorbent), a dropper, a beaker of water, a protective covering.

Challenge: "What happens if you put a drop of water on the surface of these things? What do you think? What might happen? How could we test your idea?"

Talk about what to do, and what items the learner needs in order to try out their idea, prompt them to plan and do the investigation.

Ask: "What happens? Does the water stay, or is it soaked up? What does the towel, piece of polythene, waterproof paper look like?" (Use prompts, "Does it seem to disappear?") "Is it the same for each item you tested? Can you think of an explanation?"

Introduce the word 'waterproof'.

Fair test

You can show them how to make waterproof paper by colouring a patch of non-absorbent paper with a wax crayon.

Ask if the piece of paper that they have crayoned is waterproof. What about a piece of the same paper they have not crayoned? Why must the two pieces of paper be the same kind?

I'm waterproof!

Ask: "What happens if you put a drop of water on the back of your hand and a drop on a piece of kitchen towel?"

Note predictions or what the learner says. Ask what things they need to test their idea and what they will do with the items, thus making an action plan.

Ask: "What did you find out? Are the results the same as your prediction?"

Work though the activity.

Ask: "What has happened? What have you found out?"

If they don't remember, have them soak their finger in warm water for a few minutes whilst you make up a rhyme/read/play/sing about body parts, such as the 'Head and Shoulders-Knees-and-Toes' song, available at http://kiboomukidssongs.com/head-and-shoulders-knees-and-toes-song-and-lyrics/.

Ask: "What does your skin look like when it has been in water? What happened to the sponge/paper – did it look the same when you took it out of the water? What happened to it?"

When the learner has talked about what happened to the sponge/towel, invite them to talk about their finger and what the difference is. Prompt children, asking if the water has done the same to the finger as it did to the paper/sponge.

Blobs on my skin!

Revisit or introduce the word 'waterproof'. You could have a wellington boot sitting in water and show that it is dry inside, then ask how we could describe this phenomenon.

Ask: "What other things do you know that are waterproof, like a wellington boot? What clothes do we wear to keep water out? What other things do we use to keep dry?"

Challenge: "What happens to a drop of water when it goes on your skin? How could you test your idea? What can you do?"

Encourage the learner to devise an investigation. Suggest the dropper or using a straw to deposit a drop of water on the back of their or your hand. Was their prediction found to be accurate or not?

Keeping cool keeping warm ! Clothes for the weather

Show some pictures of different kinds of weather: sunny hot day, snow and ice, rainy, overcast.

Ask the learner to describe the weather today and what clothes s/he is wearing. Does s/he feel warm, hot or cold?

Show pictures and name different clothes.

Challenge: "When would you wear this? Does it help to keep you warm or cool?"

Clothes

Show these real things or pictures. Talk about them:

sunglasses, wellingtons, PE/play clothes, mittens/gloves, scarf, umbrella, short socks, big coat/anorak, bobble hat, shoes, hoody, swimming trunks/bathing costume, flip flops, sandals, trainers, woolly jumper/sweater, shorts, sun hat, goggles, summer dress, long trousers, vest, long socks, T-shirt.

Challenge: "Can you group these pictures into hot weather clothes, cold weather clothes, wet weather clothes?"

Ask: "Are there are any clothes you could wear all year round by themselves or with other clothes?"

Moving

What can I do?

Ask the children what they can do.

How do they move from place to place?
How do they pick things up? Put on their clothes?
How do they eat food? Drink liquids?
How do they communicate with each other and you?

Moving from place to place on the ground

Challenge: "How do you move from place to place, using your own body? How Many ways can you think of? Show me or tell me!"

What is their answer? Walking, running, hopping, jumping, crawling, bottom shuffle, sliding on feet, sliding on floor, rolling, hand stands?

Ask: "Which method do you use most often?" "How do you move in water?"

Challenge: "What part of your body do you use most often in moving from place to place? How can you check? Let's list the different ways!"

Ask after this practical activity: "What makes you move? What do you do with the part of your body that touches the ground?" *(They use their muscles to push against the ground.)*

Ask: "Can you show me how you push when you walk? Which part of your foot does the pushing? What happens if you walk on your toes, not your whole foot?"

A walking talk

Ask: "Can you walk five steps slowly and tell me which leg is pushing and what the other leg does? Does it stay still or does it move?"

Can you make up a chant of what happens when you walk? Such as:

> One and . . . . . . Push left foot.
> Two and . . . . . Keep on ground right-foot.
> Three and . . . . . Pick jump right foot.
> Four and . . . . . . Bend right knee.
> Five and . . . . Move right leg to front.
> Six and . . . . Put down right foot.
> Seven and . . . . Pick up left foot and start again!

Look on the Internet for songs, such as fitness songs and walking songs. There are a number of walking songs for children you could use.

One leg

Challenge: "Can you balance on one leg? For how long? How can we measure the time?"

Ask: "Do you wobble? How do you try not to wobble over? What part of your body do you use to try not to wobble over?"

Balancing

Bending backwards, bending forwards

How far did they try to go without falling?

Challenge: "Can you lean backwards and not fall over? How far can you bend, and then what happens? Why?"

Challenge: "Can you lean forwards and not fall over? How far can you bend, and then what happens? Why?"

Can the children feel that there is a point where they start feeling they will over balance? What do they feel they need to do to stop the feeling? Can the children explain that there is a point where they start falling?

Other movements

Challenge: "Do other parts of your body move sometimes? What can you think of?"
  Perhaps they mention breathing, drinking, eating, dressing, playing.

Breathing movements

Ask them to sit and think about any movements they can feel even though they are not moving from place to place, locomotion. Suggest they feel their chest by putting their hands on either side of their rib cage. Demonstrate the position to them if necessary.
  They might realise that their chest is moving up and down. These are the breathing movements to draw air in and push air out with the water from their lungs.
  Ask: "Can you tell me what this movement is? How many do you make in 30 seconds, how can we find that out?"
  Challenge: "Does your chest change size when you breathe in and then out? How could we tell?"
  Ask: "What would we need to measure the change in chest size?"
  What do the children suggest to measure the change in chest size? What will you suggest?

Change in chest movements

Challenge: "Is the chest moving rate always the same?
  Ask: "Do you know any way we can increase the number of chest movements you do? What do you think?"
  Talk about what they feel like after running round the playground. Does that affect their chest movements?
  Ask them to sit down for a minute and count the number of times their chest moves up.
  Challenge them to count the times; you count too whilst timing a minute with a stop watch.
  After talking about this, ask them what happens to their chest movements if they jump up and down on the spot for a minute or perform some other activity. Then ask them to sit down and notice their chest movements.
  Ask: "Are they the same or different? Why do they think they have changed?"
  Ask: "Do you feel different when you have had exercise like that? What has changed?"
  Cue children into thinking about what they observe in themselves – breathing rate, deep breaths, their temperature, are their clothes too hot?

Hands

Picking things up movements

Ask children how they pick things up. Which part of their body do they use?
  Ask them to show you how they pick up three things that they can select for themselves. Can they name them? Describe their shape? Ask them why they chose

these things. What can they say about picking them up? Did they find it easy to pick the item up with one hand or did they need to use two hands?

Challenge: "Can you lift the items up using a different part of your body? How can we record what you find out?"

If children do not suggest a way, suggest they try the activity. Then talk about how they can keep a record.

Pick up activity

Have a pencil, a small book, a cup, a ball, a plastic knife, an eraser, a ruler, a safety pin, plastic coin on a table.

Encourage the child to pick up each item, ask them what part of their body they have used.

Talk about it, did they say 'hand'?

If so, ask which part of their hand. Was it always all their hand? Did they sometimes use just a bit of their hand like a finger and thumb?

How did they pick up the very small items? The big items?

Try the activity again: Pick up 2!

Suggest they keep a report by having a chart. They may like to draw the items in the left column. How will they show what part they used? Do they think of putting a tick?

Do the children work out that they always use their thumb but not always all their fingers? If not cue them; count the ticks on the data chart.

Table 5.1 Picking up

Item	One hand or two?	Use all hand (all fingers and thumb)	Use thumb and a finger	
Pencil				
Small book				
Safety pin				
Chair				
Cup/beaker				
Bean bag				
Plastic knife				
Eraser				
Ruler				
Waste bin				
Coin				

Pick up – no thumb!

This follows on from the previous activity 'Picking up'.

Challenge: "Can you pick up the items without using your thumb?"

Ask: "What do you think will happen? Why?"

What does happen? Is the learner able to explain? Did the finding match what they thought would happen?

Using one eye

Challenge: "Where are your eyes?" Cue them by asking, "Back of head? Side? Front?"

Ask: "How many eyes do humans have? How many eyes do you use when looking at things?" *(Be careful not to do this activity if the child has strabismus and only has monocular not stereoscopic vision.)*

Put a ruler at the edge of a table so most of it is sticking out.

Can they touch the tip of the ruler standing just over an arm's length away?

Then ask them to close one eye and try again. What happens? We need to use two eyes to judge distances. Some people only use one eye at a time and they learn to compensate in judging distances when, for example, pouring out a drink into a cup. Try that too with two eyes and then only one.

Using ears

Hearing

Ask: "What is the job of ears? How many do you have? Where are your ears?"

Challenge: "Can you tell where a noise comes from? What do you think? How can you find out if your idea is correct?"

If they do not come up with an idea for an activity to try out, suggest the following. If they do have an idea, let them try it out. Ask the child in each case, before they start doing the activity, why they think that idea will answer the challenge.

Suggest the learner sits down on a chair with their back to you. Have something that makes a noise.

Stand in front of them and explain that you're going to make a noise, then make the noise.

Suggestions for noise making could include: a bell, tapping a tin, a triangle, a drum. Agree how they will indicate from where they think the sound is coming, using positional language (e.g. in front, behind, on top, below, to the side). Ask the learner to close their eyes.

Standing about one metre away from the child, make the sound.

Draw a diagram on a piece of paper of the child (the hearer) in the centre, perhaps using a circle to represent them. Draw ear flaps in the normal position. (Ears in mammals are ear flaps; the ear is inside the head. Our real ear is inside the head; what we call ears are really ear flaps catching sound to channel it to the actual internal ear.) In a different colour put where the child thought the sound was coming from. Use another colour to mark where the sound was made (sound maker). Alternatively, use a teddy bear or other favoured toy animal to place where the learner thinks the sound came from.

Does what the hearer thought agree with what the sound maker did?

Table 5.2 Food chart

Name of food	Bought? From where?	Grown by you?	Hunted by you?	Plant (P) or animal (A) origin	Name of animal or plant	Eat cooked	Eat uncooked (raw)
Milk							
Cheese							
Egg							
Bread							
Apple							
Crisps							
Burger							
Orange							
Baked beans							
Cabbage							
Chips							
Tomato							
Fish fingers							
Total							

Food

Challenge: "What do you eat? From where do you obtain your food?"

Talk about where their food comes from. Do they make their own or do they have to find it or expect someone else to find the food for them?

Ask: "Who gives you food at home? From where do they get it? Do they hunt it, grow it or buy it?"

Ask: "What food do you like best?" Do they know from where it comes? Are some of the foods cooked and some uncooked? The foods in the table are just an idea; ask the learner which food s/he would like to think about.

You may like to have pictures of the different foods to make it easier to name the foods and talk about them.

Fill in a chart on food. Tick the answers. *Do you know?*

Where does most of the food the learner talks about come from? Is it bought or home grown? Do they eat more food that is cooked (for example bread is baked)? What does the chart tell them if each column is added up? Can they 'read' the data by counting the ticks?

Table 5.3 Using parts of you

Do you use	Yes	No
Your feet?		
Your fingers		
Your lips		
All your hand		
Your nose		
Your tongue		
Your cheeks		
The palm of your hand		
Total		

Feeding movements

Fingers or forks?

You need a collection, or pictures of various items, of things that assist humans in eating such as, a straw, a beaker, a spoon, a knife, a fork, a scoop, chopsticks, feeding cup, babies bottle.

Ask: "How does food get inside you? Do you use anything to help you put food (drink) in your mouth?"

Challenge: "What parts of your body do you use in eating and drinking?"

Ask the child to mime each action to show you and work out what parts of their body they use. Record children's responses following cue questions. Tick or cross in the chart according to their reply.

What does the learner think? How do they know from the chart what parts are used? Which part do they use most often?

Teeth

Begin the activity by asking, "What do you use your teeth for?"

Use a mirror and ask the child if s/he knows how many teeth s/he has?

How many teeth does the child see in the mirror? How can s/he check? What do they suggest?

Suggest that they pretend to eat a crisp. What do their teeth do?

Pretend to eat an apple. What teeth are used?

Pretend to eat a lollipop.

Pretend to eat an ice cream.

Ask: "What different actions do you use their teeth for?" Cue them with words like biting, licking, nibbling, biting, chewing.

Table 5.4 Body parts used in drinking

Part	Drink	Action
Lips		
Tongue		
Cheeks		
Hands		
Teeth		
Other		

Drinking movements

Challenge: "What different ways are there of drinking something?"

How do you drink water from a bottle, juice from a small carton of drink? Water from a cup or beaker?

Can they think of a way to record what they find? They could draw themselves!

Do they mention hands to hold the drink?

Do they say mouth or lips, cheeks? Moving their jaw?

Draw a recording chart together that the drinker can fill when they have found out.

Using hands

You need, soap, water, a bowl, a white towel or kitchen towel for the child may wipe its hands.

Ask what happens when they wipe dirty hands on towels. If they don't know, encourage them to try the activity.

Idea: They need to wipe the one hand without using soap and water; they may need some water on the hand so that the dirt will wipe off. Then they should wash the hand with soap and wipe that on a towel. Put the two 'wipes' side by side. Is there a difference?

Challenge: "Why do you wash your hands before eating?"

What do they think?

Suggest an experiment – a fair test. It is assumed that both hands are equally dirty. You might like to get the children to make their hands 'dirty' somehow.

How can they tell if their hands are dirty? Does using soap and water make a difference to the dirt on their hands?

Ask: "What was the only thing that you changed?"

Hair colour. Is it all the same?

Point out that hair is our fur. What animals have they touched or seen that have hair that is furry?

Ask what we humans have on our head (not hats)?

Is the hair colour always the same?

Table 5.5 Hair colour chart suggestion, draw the chart for the number of heads you can see!

Number	Colour						
	Black	Red	Blonde	White	Grey	Dark brown	Light brown
1							
2							
3							
4							
5							
6							
7							
8							
9							
10							
Total							

Discuss different colours of hair.

Challenge: "Which colour is most seen in our class? How could we find out?"

What does the learner suggest?

Perhaps you can count the number of heads you can see, then note what colour hair they have.

Ask how they can record their observations.

Perhaps they suggest a chart. You could use sticky shapes like stars to stick on a chart or use a coloured pencil.

What does the observer find out? Which colour is the most/least common? Do you think we would get the same results in other groups?

Another hair challenge: "Is curly hair more common or is straight hair? How can you the observer find the answer?"

Assessment

In all the activities you should think about talking with the learner and observing how they set about the task to be able to assess their understanding of the task. Note their response and the prompts you have to give. It should be considered whether it is useful after a few days to repeat a task without prompting and see if they have mastered the concept. Note their communication skills and vocabulary, as well as manipulative skills and any comments they make about rationale and outcomes.

Activity 1

Have a picture of a dressed child. Ask the learner to point to various parts of the body, on the drawings/photograph, and tell you what they are.

Activity 2

Asked them to touch a named part, e.g. chest.

Activity 3

Ask them what they use different parts of their body to do, e.g. hand, teeth, ears, feet.

Activity 4

Ask the learner to explain how s/he can move across the room. How many different ways? What parts of their body do they use?

Keep any completed chart of your child's assessment profile.

Outcomes

The basic human understanding acquired through carrying out the activities provides a reference for considering other animals.

After carrying out the investigations about the human body:

- A learner should have an understanding of major characteristics of the human body such as the names of the external parts of the body and their basic shapes.
- They should learn that the outside of the body is covered with skin, which has fine hairs except in certain places, the head at this age, and that our skin is waterproof and warm.
- They should understand that we can cool ourselves and warm ourselves by choosing appropriate clothes to wear for the different kinds of weather.
- The learner can also find out about seeing and hearing and about the origin of their food and drink, that some foods need cooking and some are eaten raw and that different implements are used in the eating/drinking process.
- Some of the challenges provide the opportunity to observe and collect data; several challenges offer the opportunity for fair testing.
- Understanding of how humans can move across the ground is an important idea to understand and how we walk, the sequence of movements as well as learning about other body movements such as breathing movements, eating (as well as how many teeth you have!), using hands to pick up items using fingers and thumbs, which is an ability that few animals other than humans and other primates have.
- The activities enable the learner to apply some knowledge about shapes.

Chapter 6

Living things: other animals

Background

Plants and animals, including microbes and we humans and fungi, are all living things. Young children usually think that anything that moves, such as clouds and fire, are also living. They have to establish an understanding of living and non-living, which are natural occurring items such as rocks, rain, and constructed non-living objects, such as cars and dolls.

We humans are part of the living world and are animals. For the young learner finding out the three main kingdoms, animal, plant and fungi, will suffice but the notion of microbes, which are harmful, and those that are helpful is important. Children gradually learn to understand the category animal and the concepts associated with it (Hermann et al., 2012). However, their native language can cause problems, because of the everyday use of a word that is used incorrectly in everyday language according to science (e.g. Villalbi and Lucas, 1991; Palmer, 2013).

Animals cannot make their food like plants and have to find their food; some animals live on other animals and are called parasites. They take their food readymade from what another animal has obtained itself, such as tapeworms, which live in the gut of another animal, and absorb some of the food it has digested. Animals have to have something on which muscles can push and also gives a shape to their body, a skeleton. Skeletons are either internal, made of fluid like earthworms and the jellyfish group, or outside the body like the arthropods, crabs, insects, the spider groups, and an inside skeleton is nearly always made of bone except for the very primitive animal with a notochord. Animals are grouped according to how closely they are related; such grouping begins with a feature that can be seen such as having fur or feathers, four legs or six legs. Animals are divided into two main groups, in simple terms, the boned or vertebrates then non-boned or invertebrates. All vertebrates have the basic vertebrate skeleton pattern, head, four limbs and a back bone. The basic pattern is modified in some animals to animals that walk on two toes such as pigs and those that walk on three toes, like rhinos, or one toe, like horses. Other vertebrates such as cats and dogs walk on pads formed from all five digits. All animals feed on living things, ready-made food, either directly by catching another animal or eating them where they grow as plants. Plants stay still so the animal that wants to eat them goes to them; animals eaten by other animals have to be chased and caught. Some animals, like vultures, specialise in eating other animals that are dead, and are called scavengers. If animals eat only other animals they are called carnivores, if they eat plants only they are called herbivores and if they eat both plants and animals they are called omnivores.

Grouping animals

Vertebrates are grouped according to their body covering or number of limbs, for example.

Fish are cold blooded and their body is covered with scales, they live in water, have fins and lay their eggs in water. Amphibians have moist skins and begin life living in water but some, e.g. frogs, change from a tadpole as they grow up to the adult form and come out of the water but have to live in moist places, often returning to water. Reptiles, such as snakes, turtles and lizards, have dry scaly skins, live on land, and lay eggs with leathery coverings. Dinosaurs were reptiles and laid eggs. Birds have feathers, two wings and two legs, are the direct descendants of dinosaurs and have the remains of reptilian scales on their legs. Scales on the rest of the body have evolved to form feathers, which cover the body in nearly all birds except for the beak. (Birds that eat carrion like vultures are bald!)

Birds are warm blooded and their young develop in an egg. Birds' eggs have a shell. Mammals have a body covering of hair, differentiated teeth (they are modified in sea living mammals for the ancestral pattern) and develop inside their mother, fed through a placenta. Mammals (except seals) have ear flaps, which in most mammals move in the direction of a sound.

Animals without bones, invertebrates

Invertebrates, like vertebrates, are made of lots of cells but have no backbone. Most of the animals in the world (about 97 per cent) are invertebrates. The groups of backboneless animals that children this age will probably have seen are annelids, represented by earthworms; arthropods, whose main subgroups are millipedes and centipedes; crustaceans, (crabs and water fleas); insects (butterflies, beetles, wasps, mealworms); and the spiders and perhaps some jelly fish or sea anemones (cnidarians and two-layered animals, all the others mentioned are three layered).

Arthropods have an outer skeleton like the surface of beetles. All insects have three pairs of legs. Those with wings have two pairs (hardened to form wing cases in beetles, like ladybirds) and these wing cases are on the second part of their body. They have a pair of antennae. Caterpillars only have three pairs of true legs too; the rest of their appendages on their body are supports, called drop legs. Arachnids, the spider group, have two parts of their body and four pairs of legs coming from the front part of the body. Crustaceans, the crab group, have two pairs of feelers or antennae and more than three pairs of soft legs. Molluscs, snails and slugs, have one large muscular foot. Earthworms, belonging to the annelid group, have many segmented bodies and have no limbs.

Children's ideas

Young children gain their first impression of animals from their soft toys, from children's books, which often simplify the animals in cartoon style capturing the essence of that species, or from other media and from soft furnishings, such as curtains, and bed linen, and often depicting animal characters. They learn about live animals from those they see everyday such as pets or urban animals.

Young children recognise animals that move as living. Some animals mystify them and if they see crocodiles and alligators in particular they question whether they are real because they are not moving. They are also able to identify the features of the body of an animal if it relates to their own experience.

Two 4-year-olds at a Black Widow (spider) exhibit:

BOY 1: "I've seen one of them in my garden but it wasn't as big as that."
BOY 2: "They are not that big are they?"

A group of preschoolers at the Chinese alligator enclosure:

BOY 1: "Is that real? It's not moving."
BOY 2: "Yes it is. It just closed its mouth."
BOY 3: "There, it blinked its eye."

Children are of the opinion that animals notice them. A 5-year-old boy looked at an alligator, "It's just looking at me, it's quite unnerving."

Preschool age children's understanding of biological phenomena is influenced by personal experiences with themselves and living. Josh and Luc were intrigued with what was under the stones in their garden. They took their grandmother out to show her that there were worms and creepy things (centipedes). In contrast, Neil remarked at a tiger exhibit that the animal was just like Timmy (his cat) at home!

Words

Mammals, fish, reptiles, amphibians, birds, feathers, scales, moist skin, four legs, two legs, wings, fins, teeth, camouflage, vertebrates, invertebrates, boned, non boned, skeleton, exoskeleton, legs, joints.

You need

Mealworms in a covered container if possible (obtainable from pet shops) to observe arthropod characteristics of larvae, pupa and adult (imago); pictures of various animals, model animals such as farmyard animals, zoo animals models; soft toys representing various animals or pictures of a variety of animals; fur material (synthetic), some feathers, some reptilian skin (e.g. mock crocodile material), an egg; some mealworm larvae and beetles if possible.

Foundation experiences

Children should be able to recognise salient features, as they do when grouping shapes. In this case they should be able to recognise and name external parts of a body such as ears, ear flaps, tail, head, legs, fur, feathers and scales. They should have had experience of grouping items and describing them and giving the reasons why they put certain objects with another (making sets). They should be familiar with everyday objects.

Aims of activities

Through working with you and talking about the suggested activities the learner should:

- Be able to recognise the difference between non living and living and once lived.
- Gain an understanding of the basic classification of animals.
- Be able to place a given animal into its major category such as boned or non-boned (has it a tail or limbs?).
- And then whether it is say, for example, a reptile or an insect, giving their reasons. This is an observation skill, one of the forms of inquiry.
- They should be able to recognise members of the same major and subordinate categories and place examples together.
- They should learn to make observations, describe and communicate them and explain them. Observing is one of the key components of inquiry science, as is researching, finding out what is not known.

Activities

Living or not?

Show the learner a few items that are not alive, such as a plastic plate, a stone, a coin, a metal spoon, plastic comb.

Challenge: "What are these things? Can you name them? For what do we use them?"

What do they reply?

Ask: "What are they made from? Do you know?"

Ask: "What do these things need in order to be here? Do they need food? Do they move themselves? How do you get them here so you can look at them?"

What are the responses?

Real animals!

Show the learner real animals if you can; perhaps looking out of the window and noticing birds. Has the learning area a pet mammal like a gerbil or hamster, or is there an aquarium? You could use a container with a lid, which contains mealworm larvae in bran. Alternatively, you could show a video clip of some fish moving, a bird flying, and a dog or horse running.

Challenge: "What are these things? Can you name them? Do they all belong to a big group with a name, what are they called as a group?"

Listen to the responses then ask, "What is different between these animals and the other objects we looked at such as the knife and stone?"

Cue them to consider whether the stone and so on can move whilst the animals can by themselves, locomotion.

Ask: "What do you and all these animals need to keep going and give them energy to move? Do the non-living things need food? Can they move when they want to? How do they move?"

Once lived

This is a little tricky. We will not get very complicated but start discussing items made from parts of once living things such as paper, wool, cotton T-shirts, oil, silk.

Once alive – fossils and dinosaurs

Most of the children will have heard of dinosaurs, Show them plastic models of some of the popular dinosaurs like *Tyrannosaurus rex*. Ask them if they know what it is a model of. Are dinosaurs alive now? (Descendants of them, like the birds with scaly legs and crocodiles, are!) Do the children know what happened to the dinosaurs?

Photograph the sorted objects for the learner's portfolio.

Fossils

Some children may have seen or heard of fossils. Fossil ammonites, which look like rather large, flat coiled snails are a common fossil in rocks or to purchase online or in museum shops. If you have obtained one show the children and ask them what they think it might be. Show pictures of trilobites in rock too if they are interested. Develop an appropriate dialogue depending on the learner's response. Some buildings have fossils in their walls. Limestone areas have fossils in the stone.

Naming

Name my cuddly toy!

Have available a few soft toys such as a panda, a bear, a cat/lion, a dog, an owl.

Challenge: "What kind of animal is this meant to be?"

When they answer, ask them what features make them say that; is it their head, their colour, the body form?

Hand the learner a few 2D shapes cut from card or the plastic shapes.

Challenge: "What shape can you find in your best soft toy animal? Which is the biggest shape?"

Ask them what animals they know of. Where did they find out about them, see them, and hear about them? Perhaps they might say on the TV, in a book, soft toy, curtain material, at home.

Ask what animals they have seen today or in the last week, at school, on the way from school or at home, for example.

Why did they name an animal (if they do, ask them how they knew it was say, for example, a cat. Why did they not say it was a something else such as a bird or a fish or a rabbit (if they know these animals)?

Have some pictures or show them on paper (books, printouts, zoo guide books) or on a computer. Ask them to tell you the name of the animal and why they say that. What features make them think the animal is whatever they say. What features do those kinds of animal have? For example, a cat has whiskers, two eyes at the front of its head and fur. Cats have noticeable sharp teeth too, a long tail and four legs.

Farm animals

Obtain a collection of toy farm animals and set them on the table.

Challenge: "Can you name any of these animals?"

When they reply, note how many they know for their profile of progress and achievement. Ask them where they found out about that animal and its name. What special features does each animal have?

Do they know where the animal is found? What does it do?

Shapes in animals

Find their shape

Ask: "What is the main shape in the. . . .?'

Ask: "What other shapes are there?"

Each activity should refresh their memory of the basic shape they have experienced and provide you with an assessment opportunity.

Have a set of small shapes. Suggest that the child looks at an animal (picture) and decides what the main shape in it is. For example, if the body is rectangular, the head is a circle, leg a thin rectangle, then the child puts the shape on that part of the animal's body in the picture. Repeat. What is the shape most often identified?

Repeat this for other animal models and for animals featured in pictures.

Challenge: "Can you make a model of an animal body by drawing shapes or placing shapes together?"

Make the shape below to start the conversation.

For example:

Challenge: "What shapes can you see in this picture? What animal does it represent?"

Ask: "What shape do you think you need to make a dog, a fish, a bird?"

Is the child able to identify and name the shape s/he chooses and say why they chose that shape and which part of the animal it represents?

Document their achievements using photographs with explanatory notes attached.

Zoo animals/exotic animals

Place the collection of model zoo animals on a table.

Challenge: "Can you name any of these animals? Why do you call it a . . . what things do you notice?"

Ask them where they think the animal lives. (By the way, lions do **not** live in jungles but in African grassland. Tigers live in Asia **not** Africa.)

Show them a globe or map and point to where the animals naturally live.

Point to the continent on which the animals do live (Asia, Africa, Australia, South America, Europe) so they have heard the names. The concept of a round world and

Figure 6.1 An animal from Shapes. What is it meant to be?

distances is rather complex to grasp but understanding the names and showing an awareness of continents and biomes is useful. Remember, tigers live in the Indian subcontinent not in Africa and there are Asian elephants and African ones, although the toy animals are usually African animals with larger ears.

Show the learner any other animal models you can obtain; there are models of some reptiles (particularly snakes) and insects.

Grouping animals

Place six hoops or metal coat hangers bent into circles or squares, or put string down in a circle on the carpet or on a table. You could substitute hoops with circlers made from wool or draw circles on a large piece of construction paper.

Put out some model animals, such as a lion, elephant, cow, tiger, horse, ostrich, chicken, crocodile, snake, goose, frog, lizard, fish (or a picture of a goldfish, for example, models are more difficult to find), a beetle, egg, ladybird, a butterfly, a hen.

Challenge: "Can you pick up animals that have something the same and put them in a circle? What will you call that group of animals? (For example, four-legged animals or animals with wings and two legs, or domestic animals, zoo animals.)

Once they have grouped the animals in one way ask them which feature they chose. Then ask if there is another way in which the animals could be grouped. What is it? Body coverings, hair, scales and feathers are obvious features. The elephant has hair but it is very scarce and isn't shown on the models so perhaps don't put the elephant out at first. Really, the learner needs to already have experienced this. Introduce the elephant to the collection if you have one. Animals with ear flaps and those without is one obvious way of grouping in which to include the elephant if you have an elephant model for the learner to observe and recognise as a species and giving reasons. Other animals to show for the child to sort could be a bird, a snake, a crab, a frog, a fish, a dog.

Special features of boned animals

Being a mammal

Show the learners pictures of a variety of mammals such as a cat, a dog, a horse, a rabbit, a squirrel. If possible, show them video clips.

Ask: "Have you ever seen any of these animals? Which ones? What did you notice about them?" Listen to what the child tells you about what and where they may have seen them. Was it at home, in the playground, at an animal park or zoo, field centre or on TV?

Challenge: "What special things do they have that no other kinds of animals have? Look at the pictures. What can you see?" Show them pictures of a fish, a reptile and a bird.

Ask: "What have these mammals (the pictures you showed first) got that these other kinds of animals do not?"

Cue the children if necessary to consider ear flaps, body covering, fur or hair (some hairs form whiskers), different teeth, nose, four legs, tail. (The last one, tail, is found in all boned animals in some form, the human tail is hidden inside at the bottom of the back!) Children may know from touching animals such as pets that they are warm blooded.

Being a bird

Have pictures of different birds, such as hen, robin, blackbird, pigeon. Again, show video clips of birds if possible.

Challenge: "What is the main shape of this animal? What other shapes can you see in the picture to do with the animal? How many shapes can you see? Is it wider than it is long?"

Ask: "Have you ever seen any of these animals? Which ones? What did you notice about them?" Listen to what the child tells you about what and where they may have seen them. Was it at home, in the playground, at an animal park or zoo, field centre or on TV?

Challenge: "What special things do they have and no other kinds of animals have? Look at the pictures, what can you see?" Show them pictures of a fish, a reptile and a bird. Ask: "What have these mammals (the pictures you showed first) got that these other kinds of animals do not?"

Cue the children if necessary to consider the answer to this question.

Listen to what the child tells you about what they are and where they have seen them. Perhaps they will mention at home, in the playground, at an animal park, or aviary, different media sources, or even as museum exhibits in a natural history museum.

Being a reptile

Challenge: "Have you ever seen any of these animals? Which ones? What did you notice about them?"

Listen to what the child tells you about what they are and where they may have seen them. Was it at home, in the playground, at an animal park or zoo, field centre, a book, toy or on TV?

Ask: "What do you notice about the animals? What covers their body? How many legs does it have? What do you think they use to move about? What do they move on or in?"

Challenge: "What special things do they have that no other kinds of animals have? Look at the pictures, what can you see?" Show them pictures of a fish, a reptile and a bird.

Ask: "What have these mammals (the pictures you showed first) got that these other kinds of animals do not?"

Cue the children if necessary to consider the answer to this question.

Being an amphibian

Challenge: "Have you ever seen any of these animals? Which ones? What did you notice about them?" Listen to what the child tells you about what they are and where they may have seen them. Was it at home, in the playground, at an animal park or zoo, field centre, book or on TV?

Challenge: "What special things do they have that no other kinds of animals have?" Look at the pictures, what can you see?"

Cue them if necessary. Do they know what these animals eat? Do they know what any amphibian babies look like? How do they know? Try asking if they know where amphibians such as frogs live. How do they know that?

Show them pictures of a fish, a reptile and a bird.

Ask: "What have these mammals (the pictures you showed first) got that these other kinds of animals do not?"

Cue the children if necessary to consider the answer to this question.

Being a fish

Ask: "Have you ever seen any of these animals? Which ones? What did you notice about them?" Listen to what the child tells you about what they are and where they may have seen them. Was it at home, in the playground, at an animal park or zoo, field centre, book or on TV?

Ask: "Where do fish live? How do they move? What parts of their body do they use?"

Challenge: "What special things do they have and no other kinds of animals have? Look at the pictures, what can you see?" Show them pictures of a fish, a reptile and a bird. Ask: "What have these fish (the pictures you showed first) got that these other kinds of animals do not?" Do they say fins, scales on body, gill cover or gill slits (not perhaps with those names), live in water?

Cue the children if necessary to consider their reasons.

Special features of main groups of non-boned animals

Filling in a table is useful to introduce the learner to recording data and interpreting tables.

Challenge: "What does the chart mean? What do you share with these other animals? What is special to their group?"

Table 6.1 Table of special features of boned animal groups

Animal name	Has it a head and body?	How many legs/limbs?	Has it ears you can see?	Body covering?	How do you think it moves?
Me (human) mammal					
Bird					
Fish					
Reptile, e.g. snake					
Reptile, e.g. crocodile					
Amphibian, e.g. frog					
Mammal, e.g. dog					
Other					

Animal walk

Take a walk around the school grounds, the field or playground or even just look out of the window.

Challenge: "How many different animals can you see? Can you count them all?"

Challenge: "How many different kinds can you see? What is seen most?"

Home animals

Challenge: "How many different animals do you see at home?"

Ask: "What are they? Where do you see them?"

In your road

Ask: "How many different animals do you see when walking in the street?"

Talk with the learners about how they can record the numbers they see and what they are.

When the data has been collected you could compose an 'Animals I see' chart. Depending on what they say you may be able to obtain pictures from the Internet or an animal magazine.

Note the powers of observation of your learner. Keep a record of their comments.

It is likely they will see common animals. In England these are likely to be mammals – cat, dog, squirrel. Birds – pigeon, robin, thrush, blue tit, duck, Canada goose. At home and in gardens they may see squirrels, cats and dogs, rabbits (as pets) and inside there may be gerbils, white rats and so on and some homes keep reptiles such as terrapins, snakes and birds such as canaries. Fish may be reported from homes such as tropical fish and frogs may be seen in gardens, especially those with ponds.

Table 6.2 My animal walk and animals seen

Location	Mammals	Birds	Reptiles	Amphibians	Fish
On lawn or park or field	Picture of dog	Picture of pigeon on roof	Picture of grass snake	Picture of frog in pond	Picture of e.g. goldfish in aquarium
By rubbish bin on path or on lawn	Picture e.g. squirrel	Picture e.g. of magpie			

Animal sounds soundscape

Take another walk or invite the learners to listen when they come to school and go home or in the playground.

What sounds of animals can they hear? Which animal do they think made the sound they can hear?

Can you record the sounds and listen to them inside and say what made the noise?

Assessment of boned animals

Fill in a Myers chart. If you recorded what they knew before the activities compare that knowledge with what they can tell you after the activities. Remember that short-term memory may make it sound as if they retain much information and skills. Ask them after four weeks what they recall by framing focused questions related to their original knowledge. Record these responses and compare them with those immediately after the sessions.

You can use a chart to help report what they say, which can be kept for reference and to measure progress.

Show them the models of a variety of animals and ask them to name the animal and say to which big group it belongs, e.g. boned/non-boned, mammal, birds, etc., giving reasons for why they make that judgment.

Animals with outside skeletons – arthropods, insects, crustaceans, spiders and centipede groups

Have video clips of some arthropods such as crabs, butterflies and spiders available and earthworms, snails, slugs, jellyfish and sea anemones. If you can obtain some mealworm beetles in a closed container to show them a beetle it is very useful. They can be obtained as larvae from pet shops. The larvae, pupae and beetles can live in a closed

Table 6.3 Grouping animals assessment

Animal shown	What child says it is	Reason e.g. boned, because it has four legs (limbs) and tail	Your notes

see-through container with bran or muesli or similar. They are popularly called flour beetles. They are not harmful.

Ask: "Can you name any of these animals? Where have you seen them or found them? What is different about them all compared with you?"

Challenge: "Look at the pictures/models. What can you see that they all have?"

You may need to cue them, for example, how many legs does the beetle have, the spider, the crab, compared with them?

Snails

Challenge the children with a picture or better still a live specimen. If a real snail is not possible, perhaps you can obtain an empty shell.

Ask: "What is this animal? Do you know its name? How does it move?"

Ask: "What are the things about it that let you say it is a (snail)?"

Have a snail shell or a life-sized picture and larger picture. Ask the learner: "How many times larger than the real animal is the snail in the picture?" Suggest they fit the small snail picture (cut out any background) into the larger snail picture.

What does the learner say? What is their plan to find out?

Measuring – animal statistics

Some children might suggest they measure across the small snail both ways, height and width, then measure the same dimensions of the large snail. Can they work out how many times bigger the large snail is than the real-sized one? They may need help with this in tangible form, say 3 cm cubes for the real snail to represent its height and however many cm cubes for your picture. If you have a number of sets of the small snail size they can be laid underneath the set of cubes of the large snail picture and the number of small sets counted. They may suggest other means of such a comparative measurement.

This is the beginning of realising the scale of diagrams.

Ask: "What would you say a snail looks like if someone asked?"

Butterfly pictures

A popular activity is making butterfly pictures, painting half the butterfly and then folding the paper in half longitudinally so that the mirror image is printed on the blank half of the paper. Draw an accurate butterfly with three parts to its body and the two pairs of wings attached to the middle part (thorax). Draw a pair of antennae attached on the front of the first part of the body, the head. Otherwise, the learners will gain an inaccurate understanding of the basic external anatomy of a butterfly.

Beetle picture

Try making a beetle picture in the same way. Ensure that the beetle half you draw has three parts to its body with a pair of antennae on the head and three pairs of legs attached to the middle part and show a wing case, its inner edge down the fold of the paper.

Spider picture

Try making a spider mirror image too. This time draw two parts of the body (the head and thorax are one as a cephalothorax, then the abdomen), a pair of chelicerae, biting jaws at the front. You may want to limit these and draw a compound eye at the front of the head, and four pairs of legs coming from under the cephalothorax.

Animal shapes

Challenge the children to look at the pictures of non-boned animals again. What shapes can they identify?

Shapes drawing

What shapes does a learner recognise in the shapes of animals? Can they draw the animal they chose using shapes?

For example, some children draw a snail, others a beetle.

Homes – habitats

Where do animals live?

Have a picture of a spider's web and a picture of a spider making a web. If you can only find a picture of three animals in their habitat use those. Ask where the animal lives so the child learns the names of the habitats.

Do the learners know where examples of the arthropod (animals with an outside covering that acts as its skeleton) live or look for food?

Have a picture of a rock pool and a separate picture of a small crab, a buddleia bush and a butterfly, wet grass with some stones and a snail.

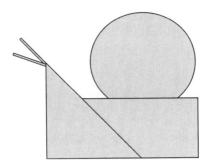

Figure 6.2 A snail

Have a picture of leaf litter and a woodlouse. Centipedes and woodlice are often found under stones too where it is damp.

Boneless animals' homes walk

If possible accompany the children outside and ask where they think they might look to find boneless animals. What sort of place would such animals live?

In the autumn where do they know or think they might find a spider's web? At other times of the year where might they see an earthworm, a woodlouse, a centipede, a slug or snail?

Other skeletons

Water skeleton!

Non-boned animals have soft outsides and water skeletons inside them.

Not all boneless animals have an outside skeleton. Some have fluid inside, against which their muscles push and pull. The earthworm groups are such an example.

Water skeleton model

Put some water in a plastic ice cube bag, a small sealed plastic bag or a sausage-shaped balloon. Ask the children to press down on the bag. Does the bag flatten? This is like a water fluid skeleton, you can push on it.

Earthworm

Obtain photographs of earthworms and real ones if possible. Make sure they are on moist leaves, sand and some soil. Earthworms can be encouraged to come up from their burrows on a lawn by pouring some soapy water on to a burrow hole. The presence of earthworms is indicated by worm casts on the surface of the ground.

Earthworm hunt

If there is patch of grass available go on a worm hunt looking for signs of earthworm homes!

Challenge: "How can we see if there are any earthworms?"

Ask the learner to plan to organise such a search. Where will they go? What do they need?

Map your findings – Make a plan

You could do a drawing of the outside of the school, a bird's eye view or on a piece of paper with a list of places in the playground or other outside places in the immediate environment; write down what animals you find. The learner could paste a picture on to their 'Animal homes' sheet or even draw what s/he thinks the animal is like.

Perhaps you could draw the basic shape of the animals you are seeking. Make sure that the correct features are shown.

'What a boneless animal looks like' chart!

Can you fill in the chart of the main features of the boneless animals you have been studying? Molluscs, snails and slugs have one muscular foot. So you could say 'one leg'.

Which animal interests the learner the most? Ask them why. Perhaps they would like to draw one?

Animal rhymes

Challenge: "Can you make a rhyme about an animal you like?"

Table 6.4 Animals without bones

Animal's name	No. of legs	Has it wings?	Outer covering	Feelers? (antenna)	Size
A spider (arachnid)					
A beetle (insect)					
A butterfly (insect)					
A crab (crustacean)					
An earthworm (annelid)					
A centipede (myriapod)					
A fly (insect)					
A snail (mollusc)					
A slug (mollusc)					

For example, see my rhymes. (Snails are both male and female, hermaphrodite so they are Mr/Mrs.)

Mr/Mrs Snail
Such as I like a snail,
It lives under a pail,
In my garden!

Mrs Spider
Where is the spider?
She's in the corner
Of the window frame
What is her name?
Hidden in a web?

Viva! Quiz for assessment

Another useful way of assessing whether the learner has understood and found out anything is to ask them.

Use some of the pictures that you have had for the learning sessions. Select say six: a dog, an earthworm, a beetle, a butterfly and a bird but have some pictures of non-animal items such as a spoon, a chair, a cup and a ball.

Place the items all face down on the table. Some children like charts so you could have a chart of two columns – animal and not animals with ten lines. Which column will you fill in and which will the learner? Who chooses? Why?

What kind of animal?

Have a collection of models or pictures of a variety of animals and some inanimate objects such as a paper clip, pencil, egg cup, book, eraser, play brick, toy car.

Make another chart but this time with two columns but the second column divided into three. The heading is 'My animals chart'. We assume the children know these representations are animals. Keep the non-animal things in the collection.

Table 6.5 My animals or not chart

An object (Adult writes the name)	An animal	Not an animal	Reason given	Comments
1				
2				
3				
4				
5				
6				
7				
8				

Table 6.6 Boned/no bones!

| Boned animals | Non-boned animals | |
	Outside skeleton	Water skeleton

Bones or not?

Along the same lines, to find out if the learner has remembered anything, pick up a picture or model at random and ask them what kind of animal it is; boned or non boned and if non-boned what kind of skeleton does it have? Fill in what the learner says on the chart. Have the non-boned animals column subdivided into two columns, outside skeleton and water skeleton.

Have some sticky stars (or a stamp) to stick in the appropriate columns of the learner. You could have a column of animals again in case the learner cannot recall what kind of skeleton the animal in the picture had. Name the animal correctly. You could have one big chart for all the naming activities.

Finger fun for remembering the main animal groups

Use your hand or the learner's. Write on small sticky labels the names of the major boned animal groups.

MAMMAL; BIRDS; REPTILES; AMPHIBIANS; FISH

Stick one on each finger starting with MAMMAL and ending with FISH either on the thumb or little finger depending on where you started. It is fun to write the names on the fingers and thumbs of children but only if the writing will come off and no one will be upset. You can find tiny pictures of a representative of each group and stick them onto small pieces of card and stick them somehow onto the children's fingers! This idea is modified from that of a Portuguese botanic garden educator, Ana Caterina Tavares, who thought of the activity for the plant groups (see Chapter 7).

You may make up a rhyme to help the learner remember. Try mine!

Little finger is fish
Hello fish!
Finger no. 3 is for amphibians,
Frogs, toads and newt

Isn't that cute?
Reptiles are on my longest finger
Snakes are long. Don't linger!
Birds are Pointing finger number one
Mammals are on my thumb.

Assessment

A check of big ideas

Rationale

Dinosaurs or a fossil in a stone or insects in amber, for example, once lived, whereas a stone or a mug never did. Don't use items such as a pencil that have a part that came from something that once lived (wood in this case). It is far too complicated perhaps at this early stage of learning.

You need a collection of models, objects and small pictures to represent members of each category.

On a large piece of paper, such as construction or sugar paper, draw a line dividing the paper into two equal halves. Write 'Living' at the top of one side and 'Non-living' (never alive) as the heading of the other half. Then ask the learners to place the items in the appropriate place on the chart and tell you why, and photograph their solution.

Ask the learner to choose an example of something alive now and that once lived and tell you about them. Can they select a 'never lived' item and explain it?

Encourage them to explain why they have put each item where they have. What makes an item living and what makes an item non-living?

Ask them to explain animals with bones and animals without.

Ask them to choose a picture of an animal and then tell you the shapes that they can see on its structure.

Outcomes

After working through these challenges with you the learners should:

- Be able to recognise the difference between non-living, living and once lived.
- Have an understanding of the simple characteristics of animals that we use to group them and be able to classify animals in their phyla and know names of some smaller groups like dogs, butterflies.
- Children should be able to justify the grouping that they give to an animal, such as it is a mammal because it has hair. It is bird as it has feathers and a beak. It is an insect because it has six legs. They should be able to recognise members of the same major and subordinate categories and place examples together.
- After the experiences they should be able to make observations, describe and tell you about the animals and the things that they notice about them and explain them to you. Observing is one of the key components of inquiry science, as is researching, finding out what is not known.

Table 6.7 Is it a living thing?

Living now	Once lived	Non-living – has never lived
Comments		

References

Hermann, P. A., Medin, D. J. and Waxman, S. R. (2012) When humans become animals: Development of the animal category in early childhood. *Cognition*. 122 (1), 74–79.

Palmer, I. (2013) The recognition and naming of plants and animals by 4 year olds from differing backgrounds in an English Foundation Stage learning area. *Journal of Emergent Science*. 6, 12–19.

Villalbi, R. M. and Lucas, A. M. (1991) Concept of 'animal' –of context. *Journal of Biological Education*. 25, (3).

Chapter 7

Other living things: plants and fungi

PLANTS

Background

Plants are essential for all other life forms; they use the energy of the sun captured in their green parts to make their food, which also needs minerals, which are absorbed from the soil by their roots and transported up the plant through tubes. The products of this food-making process (photosynthesis) are distributed around the plant from the production point in another set of tubes, phloem.

The main groups of plants are those with tubes, vascular plants, and those without, non-vascular, which are mosses and green algae mainly and have no leaves, stems, roots and can live in water, like the seaweeds. The tube plants are land livers, ferns, which don't have seeds but spores, and the seed makers. The seed makers are divided into flowering and non-flowering plants. The flowering plants are the herbaceous flowers,

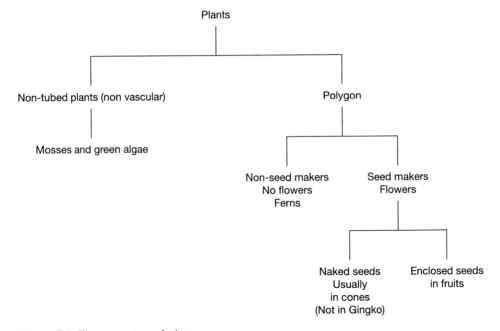

Figure 7.1 The grouping of plants

bushes and trees except for the conifers (the gymnosperms), which make seeds but no flowers. The seeds are found between the leaves or 'scales' of their cones, whilst the flowering plants produce seeds in flowers. These flowering, seed-making plants are divided into two according to the number of seeds leaves they have in their seeds – they are called monocotyledons, one seed leaf (e.g. sweetcorn) and dicotyledons, with two seed leaves, (e.g. peas). The two parts of the pea can be seen if you look at a bean or pea; the two sides of the seed, which come apart, are the seed leaves. The white stalk-like bit between them is the embryo.

Fruits contain the seeds of seed bearing plants. Many of what adults refer to as vegetables are in fact fruits with seeds inside, marrows, tomatoes, cucumbers for example. On the other hand, apples and oranges, grapes and bananas, for example, are fruit and that is what we call them in everyday life.

Fungi are more closely related to animals than they are to plants. They are not green and do not make their own food as do plants. Nor do they have the rigid cell walls that plants are made from. They obtain their food as do other animals from other organisms but don't move after food like many animals but live on another organism, alive or dead, and absorb the nutrients through very thin threadlike structures, mycelium, which form upon their bodies. They reproduce by spores so do not have flowers or seeds.

Children's ideas

Children will look at plants but are easily diverted unless there is a hands-on activity like popping a closed flower of a fuchsia, popping a full pea pod, blowing on a fruit head with the fruits containing the seeds attached to a parachute, as in blowing a dandelion clock. Very young children often investigate flowers by pulling off their petals but can watch fascinated if a bee lands on a flower. They will stroke leaves, particularly if they look 'furry'.

Children usually make very direct observational comments about the structure of plants.

A 5-year-old girl remarked, in a garden standing by a flower bed, "A flower, it's got a flower!" with great excitement, whilst a slightly older girl in this same garden said, "A prickly flower, a rose!" and added, "It's got some green bits but it's pink!" A 4-year-old girl observed, "That's a flower plant" (a daisy in flower, but remarked about the tall rose bush with pink flowers and called it "A flower tree").

Children, and most grownups, consider that large items are trees but they do notice very obvious features such as pine cones and some children in countries where it is the custom to have a conifer as a Christmas tree may, if this festival comes when they are very young, call all trees and bushes a Christmas tree until they learn to differentiate between them. People in general regard vegetables as real plants. The terms fruit and vegetable are used incorrectly in many cases whilst 'weed' is the name given by some humans to plants living in the 'wrong' place according to the name.

Adults have an everyday categorisation of plants, which they pass on to children. It is not biologically accurate. Weeds, for example, are plants growing in the 'wrong' place according to adults, not a distinct scientific category, and plants are really the flowering ones, whereas trees and bushes, and herbs used in cooking such as mint, and medicinal treatments, are each another category.

An adult with two 5-year-old boys taken on a school visit to a horticultural garden, held the following conversation.

ADULT: "You can see weeds between the plants."
BOY 1: "There's a flower, there's a flower!"
BOY 2: "I can't see any red ones!"
BOY 1: "Ah yeah, I can. There!"

An older boy remarked, at a clump of plants belonging to the *Gunnera* species (Giant rhubarb), which had large prickly stems and enormous almost umbrella-like leaves: "Wow! Look at those leaves. I have never seen a plant with such big leaves!"

Interestingly, in show gardens where plants have labels one boy responded to an adult inquiring why he thought the plants had labels, "Because they've died!" Obviously, he had visited graveyards and knew of Christian headstones.

Smell is important to young children when looking at plants, particularly the herbaceous flowering ones. A boy (6 years) remarked, "Let's see what it smells like! Ugh! It smells like poo." Yet the flower was actually a rose!

If they are allowed to touch leaves and crush them, those for example of a minty herb, they enjoy doing that. They also enjoy stroking leaves with hairs on, which feel furry. Primary school children I observed at Kew Gardens in London were intrigued by the carnivorous plants, trying to put their finger between the leaves when the warders were not looking.

However, if young children are asked to group plants that are shown to them, which they are likely to have seen every day, such as daisies, dandelions, roses, buttercups, grass, moss and ferns, they tend to do so by where the plants live, their habitat. When shown plants or parts of plants that we use as food, fruits and vegetables in everyday classification, they remark if we eat them with a main course of a meal it's a vegetable, or it's fruit if we eat it by itself or as dessert. Thus, even if we call it a vegetable, such as a marrow, pumpkin, cucumber or tomato, each must be in scientific terms a fruit because all of them have seeds inside them. Weed is a name given to any plant growing where they are not wanted, like a garden border or a hanging basket. Vegetable is the name we give to parts of plants that we eat with a main course meal, whilst fruit is the name we give to the part of soft plants that we tend to eat as a snack or in desserts like oranges, apples, grapes and bananas, whereas a number of fruits are in fact, in biological terms, called vegetables, like cucumbers and tomatoes.

The anatomical features about which children comment most are leaves, flowers and fruits and a few young children mention stems, as well as any odd, unusual bits like large prickles. They do notice the dimensions and colours too! With all the children whom I have heard looking at plants making spontaneous comments, the majority also try to name the plant using everyday names.

In work done in a reception class (4- to 5-year-olds) in an English primary school that is surrounded by pine trees, when asked, "What is a plant?" some replied it was to put a seed in the soil. They had all planted sunflower seeds earlier. Those who interpreted the question as one of categorisation or grouping, said plants were flowers and when asked about grass said it was the playing field or a lawn. They had no concept that the field was made up of grass plants.

Aims of the activities

- To help children understand that plants are green.
- Plants do not move (locomote) from place to place. They don't hunt for food; they stay still and make it.
- Not all plants produce flowers.
- Plants with tubes in the side have root stems and leaves have buds off stems, which turn into flowers, which produce fruits with seeds in them.
- Animals eat parts of plants. Recognise the parts of plants.
- Recognise and name a variety of everyday flowers and their parts.
- Seeds are a part of flowering plants and are in a fruit.
- Humans have names for differing groups of plants like weeds, fruits and vegetables, we, biologists, group them differently.
- Plants have basic shapes.
- Plants need certain things such as water in order to grow.
- Seeds need to absorb water before they can start growing.

Foundation experiences

The learner needs to know basic shapes and have an idea of proportionality. What is large compared with something else and what is smaller? They must also be able to describe where a plant lives as well as have recognition of colours and textures.

They should be able to use shape templates to match to parts of plants. They need the vocabulary and firsthand experience of fruits and vegetables and to know about cooking items before they are eaten and be able to make simple measurements with nonstandard and standard units realising the need for standardisation. They should be able to use their experience of shapes to describe organisms.

Children should be able to recognise the difference between plants and animals and know where plants are found in their everyday life. They should be aware that plants are usually found in the ground where they are planted. They need someone to move them. How is this different from the animals that they see?

Talking and doing

The objectives of the following activities are to help children understand that plants are green and that not all plants produce flowers. We humans and other animals eat parts of plants and the animal world depends on them. Through looking at specimens, including fruits, seeds and what we call vegetables and fruits, children should be able to recognise the parts of plants and their job in the life of the plant as well as the parts of higher plants. Young children like colours and shapes so can learn to recognise a variety of everyday flowers, learning their names and the names of their parts. Talking about plants in the lives of children and learning the appropriate everyday words is an important part of this set of activities. Show a whole plant with stem root and leaves and flowers if possible; a 'weed' grass plant is easily pulled up and shows these parts if it is in flower or chickweed or groundsel. House plants such as *Perlagonia* (often called geraniums) or a chrysanthemum are ideal too.

You need

Examples of fruits and vegetables, real ones or pictures or plastic ones, which are often available in the home or corner shop.

Prepare a selection of leaves of trees and bushes; some real ones are ideal but pictures cut out from magazines or from photographs obtained from the Internet and printed will also do. Have some simple measuring equipment for length. These pieces of string to begin with, could be squared paper strips that match centi cubes; the learner can measure with the cubes and match to the paper strip. Rulers with large divisions can be introduced.

Also, hand lens; empty egg box cartons, dishes, plastic trays in which to collect plant parts from outside walks; seeds in packets, mung beans, chickpeas, peas, broad beans, rape and cress; dry peas for cooking, not in seed packets; cut down plastic soft drinks bottles in which to grow seeds, kitchen towel, small plastic trays or saucers on which to grow rape and cress, empty eggshells with the tops removed in which to grow rape and cress; potatoes, pictures and real examples of flowers; small whole plants such as grass plants or other 'weeds' such as groundsel to show root, stem, leaves and flower if available; some moss, ferns; breaker balance scales, plastic trays to put seeds on to weigh them; a bulb such as an onion and an old one sprouting; a sprouting potato; a small cardboard box (shoebox, tissue box or cereal packet, blacked out, with hole at one end); mushrooms; mouldy bread in a sealed see-through container; kinds of 'weeds' are usually the easiest to obtain! You could grow rape and cress or a bean to show root stem and leaves. The first 'leaves' that appear in these plants are the cotyledons, which are part of the seed. In other plants the new shoot grows real leaves when it is above ground. Pine cones, jug, water supply, kitchen towel, photographs of leaves, thin card, scissors, wire coat hanger to make the mobile frame, thin string to hang the leaves onto the mobile, card tubes (e.g. toilet tissue or kitchen towel inside tubes, paint/crayons, string, hole puncher to make a 'plant spy' tube) water, measure, compost, soil, vegetables, turnip, beetroot, carrot, potato, leek, cabbage (round), radish. A few cut flowers that wilt easily. Digital thermometer or pocket infra-red thermometer. A plant, e.g. a herb such as mint, a chrysanthemum or *Pelargonium* (geranium).

Words

Flower, stem, stalk, leaf, pollen, flower, petals, sepals, seeds, fruit, green, prickles, roots, root hairs, water, grow, seed leaves, cotyledons, absorb, weigh, weight, fair test, numbers up to ten and twenty, measure, ruler, bulb, light, no light darkness, wilt, flop, turgid.

What is green?

What colour do all plants have?

Have the learners an understanding of the concept of green? Look around the classroom, invite them to go and point out or touch items that are green in colour. What green items can they see outside when looking out of the window?

Challenge: "How many different shades of green can you find?"

Parts of plant

Ask: "What are the main outside parts of your body?" Invite them to touch the main outside parts.

What do they know are the main parts of a plant's body?

What do they say? Do they mention roots, fruits and seeds or just leaves and a flower and a stem? Do they mention trunks and branches? What kind of plant are they thinking of?

Look at bulbs such as hyacinths, a grass plant or other weeds that can be pulled up from the soil easily. You could grow rape and cress on a piece of damp kitchen towel and identify the root, stem and leaves (they may see leaves developed from the cotyledons in the seed) to show the main parts of the plant.

Draw an outline of a plant to show the roots, stem, leaves and flower. (Draw a side view of an imaginary buttercup, for example, that looks like a semi-circle.)

Ask the learners, "What are the parts of this plant? What shapes can you see on the plant?" Provide them with cut-out shapes the same size as your drawing (semi-circle, oval, thin rectangle, thin oblong, circle), wavy lines (roots) or draw a tap root as a thin upside down triangle.

Perhaps you could show them a few plants, like a carrot with its leaves. The root is an inverted cone shape, the leaves are elongated oblongs in shape.

Provide some shapes and ask them to make a picture with the shapes of a plant they know. What is each shape representing? What is the plant?

Vegetables

Have a collection of vegetables such as a potato, turnip, beetroot, leek, round cabbage, pointed cabbage, sprout, and swede.

Have a set of card shapes or plastic shapes.

Ask: "What shape is each vegetable? How can you find out?"

Ask the learner to tell you what shapes they are and how they know that.

Fruit shapes

Repeat the above investigation dialogue above but this time with fruits such as apple, orange, banana, grapefruit, grape, and mango.

How can the learner record their observations, and devise a way that will show other people which fruit is what shape?

Parts of plants

Foundation experiences

Look outside and ask children what things they can see that are green, e.g. lamp posts, waste bins, wheelie bins, street signs, front doors, cars, people's clothes.

Which of the green things are plants? Point them out to children. Give them the names of the plants. Give a superordinate human group given name like tree and a specific name like apple tree, pine tree, flower, and rose bush, daisy plant.

Explain that some plants have flowers and that trees and bushes have flowers too and make seeds. Conifers, trees with needle-shaped leaves, do not have flowers but make seeds.

Are plants always green?

Challenge: "Are plants always green? How do you know?"

Look at real plants or coloured photographs of some. What does the learner think? Talk about different plants they know.

Is a plant the same temperature everywhere?

Challenge: "Can you take the temperature of the same part of a plant inside the plant stems and leaves and on the outside? What do you think you'll find?"

This is practice at reading a thermometer, which the learners have practised in shape, space and measure.

What are their ideas? Why might there be a difference?

Is the top side of the leaf the same temperature as the lower side? (We've found that the lower side is cooler, as more water is lost on the underside.)

Under a stone

Challenge: "What happens to grass plants when they are covered up? Have you ever seen any that have had a stone or plant pot on top of the patch of grass?"

Listen to what the children say.

Ask: "How could you find out? What do you think?"

Prompt them if it is needed to consider placing a stone or other opaque item over a small patch of grass.

Ask them what their plan is. What will they use? How long will they leave the grass covered?

Photograph the grass before, then with the investigation going on, and then the grass when the item is removed.

What do they expect to see when they remove the item? Why do they say that?

What has happened to the grass? What has it not been able to have under the stone?

What happens to a green plant at night?

Can the learner answer this question? How could they test their ideas to find out? What is their plan?

Plant in a cupboard

Challenge: "Is there another way you can stop light reaching a green plant?" What does the learner suggest?

After discussion, they usually suggest in a box with a lid or a cupboard or drawer that closes tight to stop light getting in.

Ask: "Where shall we put the plant to keep out the light? What plant will you use?"

You could use some rape and cress seeds, which you have grown, a *Pelargonium* or even a sprig of broccoli (vegetable) or a herb in a plant pot such as mint (herbs in pots can be bought from many supermarkets).

Make a dark box

Suggest that they could design and make a plant dark box. What would they need to do this?

What sized plant and its pot or tray (rape and cress) is to be used in this investigation? Is the chosen box large enough to have the plant and its container placed inside?

Large cereal packets or other boxes such as a tissue box, square ones in particular, can be utilised for this. They can be 'unstuck', turned inside out and stuck back together 'inside out' and then they can be decorated on the outside. How will they put the plant into the box? What will be an opening? What can get in through that? What are you trying it stop reaching the plant (light)? (Why is this the aim of this investigation? Can the learner tell you?) What has the opening in the box to be: large or small? Why (small so only a narrow beam of light enters)?

Action!

Questions for the young investigator!

- Where will the plant and box be put? For how long will the plant stay in the box until you look at it again?
- What will happen when you open the box entrance and look?
- What time of day will you look? Why is it important to look at the same time? How can you can tell other people? Perhaps you could photograph the plant before, inside the dark box before closing it, then two or three days later, four days later and so on? Why is it important to know what the plant is like before you put it in the box?
- What do you think will happen whilst it is in the box?

Make a chart, or use the one in Table 7.1.

Which way?

Suggest that you place a potato (an old one is best) in the dark, in a box with a hole at one end.

Challenge: "What do you think will happen to the potato? Why do you think that? How long will you keep looking?"

Table 7.1 Plant in box

Plant name. . . . . . . Where it is placed. . . . . Investigator. . . . .

Days	Time	Photo or drawing	Colour of leaves of plant	Other comments
Start				
Day 1 . . .				
Day 2 . . .				
Day 3 . . .				
Day 4 . . .				
END				

What does the learner think?

Ask: "How can you make this a fair test? (Hint, two similar-sized and aged potatoes, two boxes – one without the hole.)

How does the investigator plan to record what happens? The use of a tablet or digital camera to photograph the observations at regular intervals is a useful recording means and if possible print out the observations for both boxes so you can compare them and discuss.

What does the learner say?

N.B. This takes time! This is an extended investigation, over several weeks.

Thirsty plant

Challenge: "Do cut flowers need water? Why do you think that? How could you investigate? What do you think? What do you expect a cut flower to look like in vase?"

Listen to the learner. What do they think, why do they think that? How can they devise an investigation to find out if a cut flower does require water to stay upright, like it is when put in a vase? Is the vase empty when it has a bunch of flowers in it?

What do they plan? Do they make it a fair test with a vase with water and a vase without and two similar flowers, one in the vase with water and one in the vase without? What will they look for? What do they find?

This is a very useful investigation to look at a control, observations and outcomes that can be explained and recorded with drawings of before and after or a photograph.

If the learner suggests a different kind of investigation, encourage them to carry that one out, planning it and doing it, what do they find? Cue the learner into a fair test with and without water but using the same kind and size of flower.

Talk about a leaf

Collect some leaves; start with the same kind if possible. The leaves can be from a deciduous tree (broadleaved) or from a conifer, or from a herbaceous plant such as a house plant.

Hold up the leaf and ask the child to describe it in terms of shape, size, colour thickness, or anything else. Hold up a small piece of white paper, or coloured paper, and ask the child to describe the piece of paper. What is similar between the leaf and paper and what is different?

Leaf shapes

Obtain photographs of different types of leaves showing different shapes. There are coloured photographs of different leaves on the Internet, which can be downloaded, printed out, cut out and pasted onto card.

Challenge: "What main shapes can you see? Can you match a shape to the leaf shape?"

You may be able to collect real leaves for this exercise.

Maths and leaves!

Challenge: "What shapes can you find in leaves?"

- A horse chestnut leaf is basically like a number of ovals, which join at one end.
- A privet leaf is an oval.
- A blade or leaf of grass is a long oblong with a triangle at one end.
- An elderberry is many small lobes on either side of a main line.

Some leaves are basically very round, a gingko is basically triangular, and the seed leaves of rape and cress are basically circular. Round leaved mint has round leaves. A spider plant leaf is the shape of a very long thin triangle!

Some leaves are a mixture of shapes.

Make a chart of the leaf and underneath make a replica of that leaf with shapes cut out and stuck below the shape of the actual leaf or a photograph of a real leaf.

Leaf-shaped mobile

Invite the children to choose pictures of a leaf that they like. Why do they like that leaf? Of what shape does it remind them?

Paste each of the leaf photographs on thin card and cut out the leaf with a border of card in the shape the children thinks is most like the leaf.

Challenge them: "How can you make a mobile of leaf shapes? What do you need?"

Then make a mobile!

Water

Challenge: "Do plants really need water? How could you find out?"

What is the action plan? How can they make their idea a fair test? They could use the same kind of plant, of the same size. Measure the amount of water you put in the cup with only the one flower in it.

Tubes

Challenge: "Is there a way you could show that a plant has tubes inside that carry water to all the parts (leaves, flowers, fruits, upper stem)?"

What are their ideas? What do they plan to do? Food colouring works very well and the small stalks in the middle of a celery heart or say a white or pale flower – carnations are a popular choice. The more air that is going past the leaves the more quickly will the coloured water move up the plant. If the investigation is near a breeze the water should move up the plant more quickly as evaporation at the leaves occurs more quickly and pulls up more water.

If you use a stalk of new celery, which you cut across the bottom, you can see coloured dots, which are the openings of the water tubes.

What do the children think they are?

Below ground up!

Grow a seed such as a pea in a see-through container so that the children can see the shoot as it emerges above the surface of the soil and the root below the ground, or buy some rape and cress from a greengrocer/supermarket.

Challenge: "What can you see? Has the seed changed from when we planted it?"

Again, photographing progress is an excellent way of recording what happens.

Ask: "How has the seed changed?"

Above and below soil

If you have rape and cress seedlings or a grass plant from a flowerbed or another weed (weeds are plants that grow somewhere where humans don't want them!), pick some out of the pack and lay them on a piece of white paper.

Challenge: "What parts of a baby plant can you identify/see? What do you think was below ground? Why?"

If they are a little vague, point in turn to the root, shoot and seed leaves and ask about their colour. Do they know what the baby plant needs to develop the green leaves?

Ask them to describe the colour and shape.

Parts of a plant

If possible, pull up a weed in the garden. What part of the plant was above the ground? What was below?

Ask what parts of the plant they can see above the ground and then when a plant is uprooted (or the seedling placed on a piece of paper so you can look at it). Where is each part (root, stem, leaves)?

Lawns

Many children think that the word 'grass' is synonymous with lawn, not realising that a lawn is made up of many small grass plants. Examine a lawn and let the children work out that it is not one big green plant but many little plants together.

If you can find a grass plant that has not been mown down but has developed its flowers on a long stem show that to the children. They usually do not understand that grass plants have flowers too and produce pollen (a fact known to many hay fever sufferers).

Cones

Young children in my experience seem fascinated by cones from pine trees. Pines trees do not produce flowers like flowering plants do to make seeds. The cones have seeds between their scales. Young cones are green and smooth but the older cones, when the seeds have developed, are brown and the scales open so the seeds can get out.

If you have pine trees take a cone walk. If not, you may be able to obtain cones yourself or obtain pictures from the Internet.

Children can sort and make observations about the collection.

Plant spies!

Take a plant spy walk – an expeditionary walk around the setting or school.

Have the children make a plant spying tube from a kitchen towel roll.

They can point their plant spy tube at different parts of the ground that they can see. Have they seen a plant? Is it a plant? Why? Do they know its name?

Table 7.2 Cone collection

Cone's name. . . . . . Where it is placed. . . . . Investigator. . . . .

Cones	Cone sort	Cone sort 2	Other comments
Where found			
How many?			
An example, the real thing, or drawing or photo			
Sizes – biggest			
Sizes – smallest			
Main colour?			

Plants bits safari

Provide the learner with a container such as an empty egg carton.

Challenge them to go on a plant safari and collect six bits of plant material, such as a bit of twig, a dead leaf, a blade of grass. They should not pick any other part of a plant off a living plant.

Photo shoot

A plant safari with a camera is an ideal opportunity to record what is growing around school. If it is made several times a year at the beginning and end of each term you can all talk about the pictures and point out what has changed and what has remained the same. Usually, for example, the trees will be there all the time but they may look different in spring, summer, autumn and winter, whereas evergreen trees will be the same. Why? What about the bedding plants or bulbs such as crocuses and daffodils? Are there daisy flowers on the grass in the winter?

Flower shapes

If children know the basic shapes, star, circle, oblong and bell (which is like an oval with a flat bottom), they may be able to recognise the shapes in flowers. What different shapes of flowers can the children see around outside or in the pot plants inside? Again, there is a chance for a photo journal or cutting out pictures from catalogues when such a plant shape has been sighted.

Make a folder of flower shapes. Make a similar one for flower colours. Fill in a table.

Starting to grow – seeds!

Show the learners some dried peas or other seeds, particularly seeds in a packet.

Ask: "What are these seeds like? Do you think they could change into something else? What and how?"

 Table 7.3 Maths and flowers – flower shapes

Shape	Name of flowers	Colours	Where found
Circle			
Star			
Two lipped			
Cup shaped			

Listen to the children. What do they suggest? Do they know that seeds grow into plants?

Show them a few fruits with seeds in such as an apple or an orange with 'pips'. Mangetout with developing peas in is another useful example, available all year round. Challenge: "How are seeds straight out of a fruit different to the ones we have already looked at?"

Starting to grow!

Show the children some dried seeds. Dried peas can still be bought in some shops, or have some packets of seeds from a garden centre or collected from seed heads of plants. They must be dry.

Challenge: "Do seeds grow whilst they are in their packet? If not, why not?"

What evidence do the children have that seeds do not start growing in the packet?

Open the packet. Put the seeds in a dish. Invite the children to look at them.

Ask: "What are these seeds like?" Cue them by saying that, for example, "This table is hard, this cushion is soft."

Then inquire whether they think the dry seeds will grow into a plant like that? How could we find out?"

Suggest that they devise an investigation to try out their idea. Many young children know that seeds are planted. If they suggest they plant in soil suggest that it would be difficult to see if the seed had started to grow.

Ask: "How can you tell if the seed has started to grow?"

What do they suggest? Ask when they think they will be able to tell if the seed is starting to grow. Suggest, if they do not, that you look in 24 hours, at the same time next day that the seeds were 'planted'.

Can they talk with you and draw up a chart for observations? What do the observations tell you?

When they have noticed (next day) that a dry seed does not grow ask what it might need and ask them how they would test that idea.

Water is the necessary ingredient. How much water? They may have ideas for trying to use different amounts of water. What are their ideas? Where will they set up their investigation?

What do they notice the next day? And the next day, and the next? Draw the seeds or take photographs of the seeds each day. How will they know which seed has what amount of water? How will they measure the amount?

Assessment

Inquire whether the learner can tell you about plant they like.

Why is it a plant? What makes it a plant?

We eat some flowers, can they tell you one?

We eat some fruits from plants, can they tell you which fruits we eat as fruit but which fruits with seeds in do we eat and call vegetables?

Outcomes

From looking at plants and talking about them and naming them and their very observable parts, including the roots of a plant they grow and eat, learners should gain a basic understanding of a 'plant'. They should:

- Be able to recognise and name the shapes that are found in plants.
- Be able to measure simple properties of a plant such as height.
- Know the simple words with which to describe plants.
- Understand that the word plant does not just mean flowers but that there are other kinds of plants.
- Understand some plants form part of the food of humans and other animals.
- Understand that without plants we could not survive.
- Understand that plants that make seeds are part of one big group of plants.
- Understand seeds in flowering plants grow into new plants and are made inside the plant in something that turns into a fruit.
- Know we eat fruits and seeds.

FUNGI

Background

The most common fungus of which children may be aware is probably the edible mushroom, often called button mushrooms, which still have a covering underneath the cap, known as the veil, which covers the gills where the spores are (which grow into new mushrooms) or they may be familiar with older edible mushrooms that are much larger and have brown gills that are exposed under the cap with the veil remaining as a ring of tissue around the stalk. Some people name all members of the fungi group with the stem and cap as mushrooms. Children may be familiar, probably through illustrated books, of the Fly Agaric fungus. This is the most commonly portrayed, and often mistakenly called a toadstool; it has a cap that is bright red with white spots and is poisonous but often depicted in fairy stories. Other fungi are ones such as puff balls and ink caps and small toadstools, which may be seen as fairy rings on lawns at certain times of the year. Fungi do have roots and are made of strands of tissue called mycelium. Take a stalk of an edible mushroom and pull it to pieces. They do not have tubes inside them like vascular plants do. They are not green either so do not make their own food but are parasites and live off the nutrients of others (and sometimes animals, including us). A fungus causes the skin disease in humans called ringworm, for example. Other fungi spoil food such as on mouldy bread, whilst other fungi are useful in food production such as blue cheese, yogurt and beer, as well as in bread making – yeast is a fungus.

Children's Ideas

When shown a mushroom many young children in England recognised them, "I eat them". A 7-year-old boy reconsidered and named one remarking, "I know because it's the shape, the top and the colour and my mum cooks them!" Several 5-year-olds remarked that it was a mushroom because they found out at home as their mum cooked them! One child told me that mushrooms were white and grow on the ground. It has a shape like a circle all around it. Another early years' learner remarked that they have a round bit on top, a stalk and smell. Rhys said, "It has a blown up bumpy bit and a stalk, a fat bit and a soft bit! And they grow at home in the field."

Vocabulary

Cap, stalk, veil, strands, mycelium, gills, parasite.

You need

A plate, pointed knife or sharp pencil, button mushroom, cap mushroom, mushroom stalk, damp pieces of bread, a piece of bread in a polythene bag, piece of blue cheese, mouldy apple (in a see-through container with a lid).

Foundation experiences

Talk about mushrooms and toadstools. Have the children heard of them? Have they seen any? Where? Do they eat mushrooms?

Look in some storybooks for pictures of fairies and toadstools.

Do the children eat things that have connections with fungi like blue cheese and bread, which is often made with yeast, which is a fungus? Have they seen mouldy bread or an apple?

What is this?

Show them the button mushroom.

Ask: "What is this? Have you seen one before? What is it like?"

Listen to the words they use. Encourage them to compare with those used in the next observation activity.

Ask: "Is this a plant? If not, why not, if so, what?"

Listen to their answers. This is an activity that practices observations and linking previous experience and information to describe another item.

Grown up mushroom

Repeat the above with a larger cap mushroom. Listen to the description. Write down their words. Compare them to the ones for the button mushrooms.

Ask the learner what is the difference between the two mushrooms. Can they think why?

Strands!

"What is inside the mushroom stalk?" How could the learner find out? Listen to the learner's ideas, to assist them in carrying it out. Many children suggest that you look inside the stalk. Either carefully open the stalk yourself to show the strands or let them try.

Ask: "Is the inside of the mushroom stalk like or unlike that of a plant such as celery? Can you explain?"

Have a piece of celery cut across to show the vascular bundles.

Gills

Show a button mushroom and a cap mushroom with the gills exposed.

Tell them that the gills are where the spores are made. Spores develop into new fungi of the kind that made them.

Ask: "How can we tell if the gills do make things?"

What does the learner suggest?

Hint

The easiest way is to use a young mushroom where the veil has just broken; cut as near to the top end of its length as possible and put the cap gill downwards on a piece of white paper and leave for a couple of days. When the learner removes the cap they should see the pattern of the gills in black powder, the spores.

Interpretation question

"What does the pattern mean?"

Assessment

Show some illustrations or real specimens of some flowering plants, and some mushrooms.

Can a learner describe the difference between the mushroom and plants?

Did they notice that the mushroom is not green; can they work out what that means?

Ask them why fungi are not plants.

Can they recall why plants are green and what can they deduce from that information?

Can they talk about that which they have seen?

Outcomes

Learners should be able to:

- Explain the differences between a plant and a fungus.
- Know fungi are not green.
- Know fungi are made up of thin strands.
- Know from where the fungi obtain their food.
- Know fungi do not make seeds.
- Know some fungi are edible but others are poisonous so only eat those bought in a shop.
- Be able to describe the shapes in a mushroom.
- Know fungi can grow on food left out.

Chapter 8

Pushes, pulls and bounces

Background

This chapter covers essential basic physics observations: forces – including magnetism –, as manifested in the experience of children, and light through reflections that often 'bounce' back in a changed direction and always in straight lines. Sound is vibration that pushes waves through the air, and we hear sound when these vibrations push through on our eardrum. These are very simple ideas, but the observations of these phenomena are essential prerequisites for later conceptual development in physics and design technology and engineering.

Forces are pushes and pulls. We use forces a lot every day, such as friction, so shoes with a good grip don't slip. We walk up a ramp rather than straight up a slope. Forces make things speed up and slow down. Items in playgrounds such as playground swings, slides and see-saws show forces in action. We feel a force when the wind blows. It moves things. A magnet is an object made from a material that produces a magnetic field that is invisible. A magnet, because of its magnetic field, attracts or pushes away, repels another magnet, and pulls items made of iron. White light is made up of different colours called the spectrum and can be split into the ones in the rainbow. Light bends when it passes from one see-through medium to another. Children can explore these basic features through simple investigations they can design.

A force is used when we open or close things such as doors, drawers and cupboards. Sometimes we use a force like a push, whilst some things like opening a casement window with the straight handle are a pull upwards, lifting up something from the floor is a pull. Forces always act in a straight line too, like a handle is pushed down to open a door, whilst some things have to be twisted to work, like the lids of some bottles and jars. The object keeps moving and, if no other forces are applied to it, or the force stops, like when you have pushed down the door handle and opened the door, whatever is pushed or pulled keeps moving at the same speed and in the same direction until the energy it has appears to run out and it apparently stops.

Every force action has an equal and opposite reaction, for example, when a ball is rolled over a smooth surface and a similar ball over a very rough surface with bits sticking up. These make it rough or less smooth, so the ball uses some of the energy from the push in getting over theses bumps. The ball on the smooth surface moves more quickly and further because the other surface 'takes out' the energy as the ball moves over the rough surface; this is friction. The surface provides a force that 'pushes back'; this is called friction. The wind is a force of air, sometimes it is very strong. Humans use this wind force to power some machines like windmills and sailing ships or to fly kites. Some flowering plants use wind to send their fruits and seeds away from the parent plant in seed dispersal whilst some plants like willow trees and grasses use the wind to pollinate their own kind.

Simple machines use forces to make moving things easier, less work. Levers are used to make a heavy object move, like using a stick to push up a stone from the ground to see what is underneath it or pushing up a lid from a tin. When a child sits on a see-saw near the middle of the see-saw and moves an adult sitting at the end of the other end of the see-saw, they are actually using and noticing the effect of levers.

Ramps make it much easier to walk or push from one level to another. Ramps are built in the side of steep hills instead of going straight up, often they zigzag, which is lots of short slopes one after another. A ladder is a ramp when it is leaning against something, like those in play frames and a slide in a playground is effectively a shiny ramp. Children can feel the vibration at the front of their neck when they speak. If they make a plastic comb into a musical instrument by covering it with paper, waxed or greaseproof or glazed paper is best, their lips tingle with the vibration when they try to put it between them and make a noise with it. Alternatively, you could spread paper tightly across the open end of a container, pour rice grain on and tap the size of the container to make the rice jump!

Children's ideas

Children, particularly pre-school and through their play, are intuitive scientists observing, testing and remembering what happens and usually repeating the action again and again (collecting experimental data!).

Up down!

A 2-year-old girl, Thaj, sat by a power socket switch patiently pushing the switch up, then down. When there is an external observable outcome of their action like making a light switch go on and then off as they push the switch up and down, children are even more pleased.

Torch

Josh, when aged 5, found a torch, and worked out what was the switch; he had the strength to switch the torch light on, and off, and shine it. A child has to switch something on and off – it seems very satisfying to them. Josh had another small torch and switched it on and shone the beam of light across the plain dining table. He noticed the beam of light was straight. He then said he was going to shine it at me but was curious that the light beam, even though he wanted it to, would not reach me because it was only straight and he didn't move the torch directly in front of me. He eventually announced that the light would only shine in a straight line.

Reflections

On another day he found that he could reflect light from the blade of a blunt knife into his brother's face, still in a straight line, but he could move the blunt knife to direct the light to where he wanted it to go! Light travels in straight lines, but effectively bounces off a surface to elsewhere.

The force!

Daniel had two magnets that he tried to put together and was amazed that he could not push them together, but if he turned one round they almost snapped together. He tried and he tried and eventually said there was a force that stopped it but magnets were meant to stick to things, like the metal fridge door. He had found that magnets with the same pole brought together repel each other.

Children know about pushes!

The following transcripts are from the actual conversations of 6-year-olds who had been invited in a group of six pupils to come and observe some live animals. These were mealworms, *Tenebrio sp.*, larval, pupae and the imago (adult beetle) kept in a see-through container in which they live in bran, with a few pieces of fresh potato or lettuce to provide moisture.

Don't push me! The learners realised that in order to move the animals were pushing against the bran.

BRYAN: "Luke don't push me, Luke . . ."

They looked at the mealworms in a container.

LUKE: "This one is pushing, it's moving . . ."
BRYAN: "Hum . . ."

Up and down!

When Lily was two and a half she went to her cousin's birthday party, where she was given a helium-filled balloon with a piece of string attached. She enjoyed this and experimented with letting the balloon move upwards until the string was taut, then she pulled the balloon down again. This activity kept her engrossed for a long time as she walked around the room showing everyone who would pay attention that the balloon went, "Up! And down, up and down." She enjoyed a pull as the balloon floated up and the pull she could give to pull it back down!

The see-saw investigation

A boy, Jonathan, realised that the task set was similar to the see-saw when the child can move an adult sitting at the end of the see-saw (the lever) upwards. The child's thinking is aided by a reflective toss question, and then the next question contains a further challenge.

JONATHAN: "The task was that we have 5 g on one side and 10 g on the other side of the balance. . . . and we had to get the 5 g to lift up the 10 g. If you are on a see-saw and you weigh the same as each other it won't go up and down unless you push.

TEACHER: "What are you going to do with the masses then?"

JONATHAN: "I am going to do the same as you do on a see-saw. You have to move the 10 g or the 5 g into the middle or outwards so that you can make it balance. The 5 g is light so put it at the end and the 10 g is heavier so put it near the middle."

TEACHER: "Can you make the 5 g move the 15 g now? Work it out. What have you got to do? What did you do last time? What did you do with the heavier masses?

JONATHAN: "You had to move it in or out and the 5 g moves the 10 g, the heavier one? Put it nearer the middle!

Some children missed the point of the exercise and were at level 2 – level 1 being just setting up the balance.

Gemma said: "When we set up the ruler with cotton reel we had three 5 g masses on one end and 5 g on the other end then we had to put them down and see what happened. I put 15 g down and it did not balance."

Balance with masses

Rhys, Amy and Nina were two years older than the children whose experiences are recorded above. The teacher was able again to 'cue' them with an appropriate question to develop their thinking. She did not tell them.

NINA: "Put 2 there and that 1 there and see if it balances (equidistant apart)."

AMY: "No it doesn't."

NINA: "So we put 3 here and 3 there."

AMY: "Take 2 on each side."

NINA: "No."

AMY: "How about 1 each?"

NINA: "No."

TEACHER: "Have you forgotten what the task was?"

AMY: "Hum what was it?"

RHYS: "To use 5 g to lift 10 g."

NINA: "That's it! Yeah!"

AMY: "Hang on a minute. This is larger (10 g) that's why it's not working."

RHYS: "How about if we put 2 here and 1 there (2 at end 1 near middle)?"

TEACHER: "So that doesn't 'work'. What could you do?"

AMY: "Put 5 that end and 10 there."

RHYS: "No, that doesn't work."

TEACHER: "Do you have to put both sets of weight at the end of the balance?"

NINA: "Yes."

RHYS: "No."

AMY: "I know, put the 5 at the end and leave 10 near the middle."

RHYS: "Yes – we done it – Let's write it."

Eureka!

Luke struggled away by himself then announced the following:

> This is Luke. When I put the thing on, 2 masses at one end and 2 at the other end, one of them went down, the 2 masses because they were heavier. When I put the 2 masses nearer the middle the 5 masses went down. When I took the 10 masses away from the middle it would stay equal.

Air out!

One party time Josh was excited to find that if he let off a blown up balloon whose neck was only held, not tied, the balloon flew around the room!

One bath time at his grandparents he was given a dry sponge. He put it in the water and squeezed – and squealed with delight as air bubbles came out!

Aims

These activities introduce the learners to physical science.

- pushes and pulls;
- the effects of gravity and air resistance on a fall;
- air is all around;
- the effect of moving air, wind and the basic principle of lift;
- that light travels in straight lines and is reflected;
- that magnets attract (pull) or repel (push) each other;
- magnets attract certain things and not others;
- that sounds are moving air.

Foundation experiences

Young children need to be able to play in their everyday environment, although adults should watch that they don't endanger themselves, although they do have to learn to estimate risk for themselves.

They should be able to hold things, pick things up and place them down and be able to pull and push, pour water and be able to control their pushes so they may give a small push, a light tap or harder push or pull. They should be able to feel with their fingers and be able to hear. They should be able to manipulate objects and pluck, for example, a rubber band. They should know right and left sides of their body and the names of the parts of their face.

Vocabulary

Force, push, pull, up, down push, pull tight, lift, balance, light, colour, bend, see through, water, straw, tin, tap, can, empty, full, half full, glass, ear, nose, touch, bounce, reflection, shadow, block, image.

You need

Round magnets with a hole, play dough, bar magnets, items that are attracted and items that are not, bottle cap, safety pin, coins, pebble, foil, rice grains, plastic spoon, plastic comb, pencil, crayon, plastic cup, glass tumbler, water in a jug, strong broom handle or shopping bags, torches, small flat mirrors, shiny spoons (dessert or serving), shiny things such as foil, shiny tin lid, large nail, another nail, rubber bands, small hollow box open at one end, sand box.

Here is a recipe for play dough, which some of us have found useful.

4 cups of water
4 cupfuls of flour
2 cupfuls of salt
4 teaspoonfuls of cream of tartar
4 tablespoons of cooking oil.

Once made it lasts in a sealed container for a long time. If you want to colour the dough add some drops of food colouring.

Activities – forces

Know your g forces

Ask: "What action do you use to fill a cup of water or juice?"
   Ask: "Which clothes do you pull on?"
   Give a ball of play dough. Ask the learner if they can change the shape. What do they have to do? Push or pull? Are they using a force?

Feel the force

What goes up and down? Forces everyday!
   What forces do the children use and see everyday? Ask them what things they push and what they pull. Why do they have to push and pull things?

Push my hand

Ask the children to hold a book on top of their hands. What do they feel? What would happen if they took their hands away? What do they think? Try with a small tray, which will not break when the children let it fall. They have felt the force pushing down on their hand.

Do you push or pull?

Have several small card tubes.

Challenge: "What happens if you push with your hand on the top of the tube standing up on the table and then push on the side of another tube lying on the table surface? What do you think will happen? Why? What can you do to find out? How can you make the test fair?"

Challenge: "What would happen if you pushed one tube very little but the other very hard? Would that be fair?"

Pull ones!

Challenge: "What action do you have to do to put on your socks?"

Ask: "Pretend to put a coat on." (Mime the action.) "What are you doing? Do you push or pull?"

What other clothes do you put on using pulls? Do you push on anything? How would you put on a hat?

Shake or pour?

Have a card box, for example several small cereal boxes. Put small items like rice grains into one box with a big opening at the top. Give the other box a very small opening or several small holes in a piece of card or thick paper covering the opening of the box or have a pepper pot.

Challenge: "What action do you do to get these things out of their container?"

Watch what they do. What happens? Can they explain? What actions do they make? Usually a child pours one and shakes the other.

Sucks and squeezes

Ask them how they squeeze toothpaste or pour something else from a tube. How do they suck up drink from a glass or carton? What happens if they blow instead? How do they get something, e.g. cereal out of the packet? Shaking and squeezing are all pulls or pushes.

Dropping things

What things go down to the floor every day? What can children point to that goes down to the floor or nearest the surface beneath them? What happens if they accidentally drop something? Where does it go? Use the language of dropping, including catching, breaking, falling, bouncing in your dialogue with the earliest of learners.

Up!

What things go up again after they have gone down? Ask the children what they think. Bouncy balls do because of the property of the material from which they are made, so do balloons filled with air or anything thrown up by the child. Such actions are working opposite the force of gravity but eventually gravity 'wins' and the items stay on the ground or whatever surface they land upon. What can the children say about when things are dropped? Do they notice a pattern? Does the same thing always drop when they let it go? This is gathering evidence and seeing a pattern.

Dropping things – air resistance

Is there a difference in how long an object takes to drop to the floor compared with another kind of object? Try dropping a feather and a pencil. The feather has air resistance so takes longer. Find pictures or a film clip of the astronaut on the moon, which has no air, who dropped a feather and a hammer at the same time. The objects landed at the same time. Would this have happened if he had done this on earth? Try it!

Down to earth

Challenge: "What happens if you drop something? Where does it go? How can you find out?"

What does the learner say? Ask if what they think always happens. How can they test that idea?

Listen to their plan. Perhaps suggest they collect a few items from around the room, for example, a Lego brick, a pencil, a piece of paper, a solid ball, a crayon, a piece of ribbon, plastic spoon.

Ask them to say what they think will happen.

Ask them to carry out their investigation. What happens?

Bouncing balls

Show the learner a rubber ball and a solid ball, the same size if possible.

Challenge: "What happens if you drop each of these balls in turn? What did you think or predict will happen? How can you find out?"

Encourage them to plan their investigation. Watch them carry it out. Ask: "What happens?"

Listen to their explanation of their result. Can they explain why one ball goes back up when it bounces? It is made of a different material – rubber.

Ask: "What will happen if you let that ball carry on bouncing?"

Can you watch and see if they are correct in their prediction?

Air

On the earth we have an atmosphere of air. We breathe in air and breathe out. We see aeroplanes, birds and insects in the air. We feel moving air as wind. Air has certain properties and takes up space. The following simple, observational and investigative experiences introduce children to the air around.

Lifting paper with no hands!

Challenge: "Can you lift this piece of paper up so it is flat out in front of your face?"

Give the learner a small piece of paper, half the size of a piece of computer paper. Ask them to hold it out horizontally and drop it. Then pick it up and ask them to describe what happens as it flops down.

What do they suggest? Let them experiment.

Cue: If they do not think of it suggest they use their mouth to make a wind by blowing across the top paper but we want the child to work that out. Challenge: "What happens if you blow across the top side of the paper held in front of your face?"

This is Bernoulli's effect – the basis of flight!

Feel of air

Challenge: "What does it feel like if you blow air on the top of your hand with your lips pursed making a blowhole? What does it feel like?" What happens if they blow on their hand with their lips?

Air blowing straw football

Challenge: "Can you blow a piece of paper along using a straw?"

Give the learner a straw and a piece of oblong shaped paper and issue the challenge. Ask: "What do you do? How do you use the straw?"

Design and make an air blower

What can be used to blow air instead of a straw? Try rolling up pieces of different paper to make tubes. Which paper makes the best blow tube?

Fan

Challenge: "Can you make a tool that will speed up how a piece of crumpled paper moves across a shiny floor?"

Ask: "From what will you make your tool? How can you make a paper ball? How will you make it create a wind?"

Ask them to choose what they need and tell you their plan. How will they test their idea?

If they succeed in making a fan, either with a flat piece of paper or folding it, test which is the most effective at creating air current. How can this be measured? Can they measure the distance a paper ball travels and how many times do they have to waft the fan for example? Thus collecting data and comparing results?

Bubbles

Challenge: "Can you make bubbles in still water with your hand?"

Ask: "What can you do to try? What do you think will happen? What do you need in order to find out if your idea works? Can you plan what you need? What did you do? What happened? Why?"

Soap!

Challenge: "What happens if you add some soap (washing-up liquid or bubble bath) to the water and repeat your investigation?"

Ask: "What happens? What is different this time?"

Light

Children know the difference between light and dark and often have experiences of shining lights!

Spoons

Challenge: "What do you see if you look into a shiny spoon? Do you see the same if you look into the other side?"

Ask them if they can describe what happens!

In the looking glass

Challenge: "What does a mirror do? What can you see in the mirror in front of you?"

Listen to the children.

Another challenge! "Can you touch your nose? Your right ear? Your left ear?"

What do they do?

Assessment: Record their actions and comments.

Light bounce

Give the children a challenge when putting out a selection of items: a book with a matt cover, a towel or piece of paper, small mirror, a spoon, a blunt knife a shiny tin lid, a mat. Make sure there is a light source.

Challenge: "Can you make any of these things shine a light back at you?"

Ask: "What can you do?"

Watch what the learner does. Can they explain what happened and what they found out? "What items let the light bounce?"

Shine a torch

Provide a torch that switches on and off easily with a switch or button control.

Challenge: "Can you bounce the light beam off something so it goes in another direction? What would you like to aim the light beam at to bounce it?"

What does the learner plan? What does s/he think will happen if s/he uses one of the objects. Where will s/he put the light source and at what is s/he hoping to aim the light beam?

This is an ideal opportunity for the photo journal.

Shadows

Ask: "Have you seen a shadow? Where?"

Listen to what they say.

Challenge: "Can you make a shadow? What do you need?"

Ask: "What is your plan? Where would you like to make the shadow? What will you do?"

Listen and watch their action. Do they realise the shadow is made when an object is in the way of the beam of light?

Extra challenge: "Can you make your shadow bigger?"
What do they say and do?
Challenge again: "Can you make your shadow smaller? What do they do?"
Make some simple shadow puppets by cutting out shapes and sticking them on lollipop sticks, pencils or strips of thick card. Make up and tell a story. Or use some toy animals perhaps to hold up between the light source and screen – make shadows and tell a story.

Sounds are noise to children

My sounds

Does the learner have special sounds that they like? What are they, and why do the children like them? Are they the same sounds for different children? Are they what you like?

Soft sounds

What sounds can be made that can be heard clearly or hardly at all?

Loud sounds

Talk about loud sounds in the day that they hear. What are their observations? Where do they hear them?

Can they draw something that makes a loud sound?

Challenge: "What have we got in the room that you think will make a loud sound? Why do you think that?"
   Give a similar challenge for a soft sound.
   Assessment: What is it they choose? Can they tell you why? How do they make the sound?

Describe a sound

Make a loud sound, such as banging a lid with a large wooden spoon, then repeat the action with a metal spoon or knock two sticks together. Crumple a piece of paper. Drop the piece of paper on the floor!
   Challenge the learner to say what these sounds are. What do they think of these sounds? Ask them to turn the other way from you so they cannot see what you are using.
   Can the learner recognise what made the sound?

Sounds around soundscapes

Ask the children if they hear any sounds everyday. What sounds can they hear in the room? Where do they come from? Talk about it.

Disliked sounds

What sounds do the children dislike? Why? Where do they hear them?

Tin can band

Can the children make different noises with a collection of empty soft drinks cans?

Ask: "What do you think? What do you need to make the sound? Will the sounds be the same or different? How can you find out?"

What do they do? What do they use to hit the can? Does the learner try to blow into a can to make a noise? Do they comment about drums and other instruments?

Different can sounds

Challenge: "Can you make the set of cans each make a different noise? What could you do? What ideas do the learners have?"

Listen and try their ideas, this is real inquiry.

If they do not consider adding different amounts of water, give them the following challenge.

Ask: "How will you plan this? What did you keep exactly the same each time? What do you change?"

If they are confused ask: "What happens if you put different amounts of water in each can?"

What do they find?

Room sounds

Challenge: "Do things around the room, like the table, chair, door handle, waste paper bin, ruler, apron, make a sound if tapped with something, like a pencil?"

What happens? Can you fill in a chart? The learners could draw each item that makes a sound according to the kind of sound, or cut out a picture and stick it on the chart.

Table 8.1 Making sounds

Item	No sound	Dull sound	Loud sound

Ring a nail!

Show the learner a nail hanging down from your hand, tied on with a piece of a string.

Challenge: "What happens if you tap the nail with a pencil? With another metal thing?"

Challenge: "What does the nail feel like when it is tapped?"

If you have a triangle this is an excellent instrument on which to feel the vibrations of sound.

Pluck a rubber band

Challenge: "What happens if you put a rubber band across your hand from thumb to the last two fingers and pluck on the band? What do you feel? What else?"

Feel your sound

Challenge: "Can you feel the sound you make when you talk?"

What do they suggest? If they do not realise, ask them where their voice comes from? What happens if they place their hand over the front of their throat as they speak?

Assessment activities – forces, air, light and sound

Dress a person

Do a drawing of an outline of a child in shorts, shirt, open zipper jacket, socks, shoes and sun hat.

Ask the child to say how the clothes are put on, with a push or a pull? How would they do up the zipper on the jacket?

Taut string

Challenge: "What happens if you try to pull something with a string attached over a smooth surface?"

Ask: "What do you think? Why do you think that? How will you test your idea?"

Ask them what they are doing. Why are they pulling? What happens if there is no string? How could they move the item?

How could they make the task easier?

Bouncing magnets

Give the learner two ring magnets with holes in them, a lump of play dough and a pencil.

Challenge: "What happens if you put one magnet on the table then bring the other one close to it?"

Ask: "What words can you use to describe what happens? What do the magnets do? Does the same thing always happen?"

Ask the learner what they think will happen if they put the two magnets gently over the pencil and slide each one down towards the play dough? Why do they think that?

Ask: "What happens? What do you observe?"
Ask: "Does the same thing happen if you turn the top magnet the other way up?"
What did they say?
Encourage them to use words such as: push, pull, float, bounce, attract, repel.

Finger and thumb

Give the learner two small bar magnets. Ask him or her if they can hold each one between each finger and thumb on each hand.
   Challenge: "Can you make the magnets join together?" What do they think?
   What happens? What happens if you turn one magnet round?
   Then turn the other round?
   Can they explain it?

Water magnet

Have a small tub of lukewarm water and some paper towels. Stand the tub on the paper to catch splashes.
   Challenge: "Can you try the same investigation with your hands and the magnet underwater?"
   What do you think will happen?
   Why?
   What happens?

Sand magnets

Have a small container of sand.
   Challenge the learner to find a bar magnet buried in the sand.
   How can they do this? What equipment do they need?
   They cannot put their hands into the sand!
   What do they suggest?
   What do they do?
   What happens?

Magic movements

Place a piece of card between two upturned books so that the card acts as a bridge. Put a magnet on the upper surface. Put a magnet on the underside and make the upper magnet move.
   Can the learner explain what happens?
   Challenge: "Does the same thing happen if you place a magnet on another kind of surface and another underneath it?"
   How can they investigate this?
   What do they do?
   What happens and what do they conclude?
   Make sure they try some thick surfaces as well.

Where is the force? Assessment

Ask the learner to go round the learning area with a magnet and find three things that the magnet can pull. What were the things made from? Ask them to tell you three things that they tested and the magnet did not pull. Why not? What were these things made from?

Ask the children how they can make a sound that you can hear: a loud sound and a soft sound. Can they explain what they did?

Outcomes

After these activities learners should:

- Be able to work out how to carry out a simple investigation, how to plan what they do, how to choose items to use and be able to use them.
- Be able to talk about what they did, what happened and what they found out.
- Understand that sound can vary in its noise level.
- Know how to make simple sounds.
- Know that a light beam goes in a straight line.
- Understand that light can change direction using mirrors.
- Know that forces are pushes or pulls.
- Know that using a simple machine like a ramp, simple pulley or a smooth surface makes it easier to move things.
- Know that air is invisible.
- Know that air moves.
- Understand that air resistance slows down the fall of some things.
- Know that things will fall downwards.
- Know that magnets will pull themselves but not others.
- Understand that magnets will push away another magnet sometimes.

Chapter 9

Changes

Background

The light in the world during the daytime comes from the sun, if the clouds do not block it, but even if they do there is still some light. At night the part of the earth where we are has turned away from the sun as it goes through its daily rotation, and so the sunlight does not reach us until dawn when our part of the earth is turning back towards the sun. However, there is some light from bright stars and from the moon depending on which of these are visible, so we are able to see. If the sky is overcast the light from these bodies is blocked. If you are in built-up area with a lot of lit streets and other sources of light, natural light is much less obvious. My maternal grandfather, in the days before cars and headlights, used to go to meetings when there was a full moon so he could see to walk on the roads. My father told me he used to put a female glow worm emitting her light in his bicycle lamp to ride down the dark country lanes where he lived. The moon seems to change shape as the month passes. Moonlight is light from the sun shining on the moon. Blocking light with something creates a shadow when the light cannot pass through.

Lifecycles of living things are the definite stages that any living thing goes through from birth to death. They all start off small and are somehow fed by their mother so they have food in order that they can grow and change into the adult form. The young larval stage may be completely different from the adult, such as a caterpillar and adult butterfly, or a small version such as a puppy and an adult dog. In seed-making plants the food is in the seeds of plants that make flowers. The group of plants called angiosperms produce seeds with either one food store (monocotyledonous) or two, (dicotyledonous); as the baby plant grows it uses up its food store. Sometimes the food store (the cotyledons) comes above the ground as the first two leaves, which turn green and start making some of the plant's food. However, they are moist when on the parent plant but dry when they leave the plant. Before they can develop they need to absorb water. The root, which emerges first from a seed, always grows downwards (under the effect of gravity) and the shoot always grows upwards, whatever way they are planted. Children also have to learn that species breed true; one kind of plant or animal cannot have babies of another kind.

It is often difficult to tell what kind of flowering plant something is until the flower appears. Flowers turn into fruits in which the seeds are contained. Conifers, trees with cones not flowers, like pine trees, make seeds but not in a fruit; their seeds are between the 'leaves' or scales of a cone. These can be easily seen in dried pine cones that have dropped to the ground.

Plants often have yearly cycles. In some countries such as England many plants called herbaceous plants die in the cold weather and last over winter as a seed whilst woody plants like trees lose their leaves as the weather gets cooler in the autumn but the leaves appear again in the spring. Plants change according to seasons in temperate climes. Deciduous trees lose their leaves in the autumn after they have flowered and produced their fruit when the weather is cooling and are leafless in winter. New leaves appear first of all as buds in the spring. In countries that have cold winters some animals hibernate and many mammals grow thicker coats for the winter. They change the nature of their fur, it being thicker in winter. Most animals have their babies in the spring so they have a plentiful food supply as the babies grow up.

As plants and animals grow up they change. Humans change too, from being a baby, through the young or child form, through adolescence or change stage, to the adult form. They show, like many other familiar animals like cats, dogs, horses and sheep, incomplete metamorphosis. In incomplete metamorphosis the young neither resemble the adult in basic body form or in the proportions of the adult body, nor do they have the secondary sexual characterises like body hair, or breasts for female humans. Most animals hear and have ear drums you can see on the side of their head, but only mammals have ear flaps and some mammals can move their ears and change the direction towards which their ear flaps are facing to catch the sound.

Water is a naturally occurring liquid that can change. It can be solid as ice, liquid as water and a colourless gas. We are often most familiar with water as a vapour in the air as steam. The clear gap above the spout of a boiling kettle is the water gas. Condensation is water reforming as liquid. And that is what is happening when you see steam. Some other things change and can change back to what they were before. Spills of water, puddles and the wetness of clothes will disappear, evaporating into the air. Melting is caused by heating, like a melting ice cream or ice lolly in the sun or the way candle wax changes from solid to liquid as the candle burns. Foods contain water so when food is frozen it becomes hard but as it thaws the ice crystals change to water, which becomes liquid again and then we can cook and eat it. Fresh food doesn't keep for very long without going 'off', becoming mouldy or starting to change or decompose in another way.

Things mixed together can be separated again by methods such as filtering. If filter paper (like coffee filters or absorbent kitchen towel) is dipped into water, the water rises up the item through capillary action and the colour changes. If the water is coloured with, say, food colouring, the colour may be separated up the paper. This is the basis of chromatography. Sometimes different kinds of solids are together in mixtures and people want to sort or separate them.

But other things can be mixed and cannot be salvaged. Oil poured into water does not mix; if stirred, oil globules are formed in the water. Some chemicals, like washing-up liquid or other soaps, when added to water and stirred vigorously at the surface will make bubbles. There is a chemical change in which materials used break down and are permanently changed into something else. Food items are cooked, e.g. potatoes change from hard to soft pieces. Things can change colour! When we burn something it changes colour; bread becomes burnt toast, with black carbon for example. White rice, which starts as hard and brown, becomes soft and white when cooked. Paper burns through black to grey ash. Soil if mixed with water becomes very runny but if left in the sun it dries out and becomes very hard. Soil is made of particles. The meniscus or 'skin' on water will support light things like pond skaters or pepper grains.

Children's ideas

Ice cubes change from solid to liquid!

Luc wanted an ice cube because he bruised his forearm and he knew that the coldness of the ice cube helped take away the pain. He just put the ice cube on his arm and sat on a stool in the kitchen. He became very upset as water started to trickle off his arm and the ice cube gradually melted away.

Thaj and a pool of water

Four-year-old Thaj spilt some water on the shiny floor. Her mother asked her to mop it up but Thaj replied that she didn't need to mop it up because the water on the floor would disappear by itself! She had noticed that when it is warm and there is a bit of water it will evaporate.

Frogspawn

The frogspawn in their garden pond intrigued Josh at 6 years old; it was jelly with dots in the middle. A few days later he was upset because the dots had changed shape to big commas, but he kept going to look and found that they had turned into little tadpoles with feathery bits and a tail; they grew into baby frogs.

Alan and baby dinosaurs

One day Alan's mother went into the room with easy chairs and lots of cushions but she could see 4-year-old Alan. Then he burst up through a pile of cushions. "I'm a baby dinosaur hatching from its egg!" he said.

Timothy and kittens

When I was teaching, 6-year-old Timothy came and told me that his mother was going to have a new baby brother or sister. "But I've asked Mummy if she will have a kitten instead", he announced, "I don't want a brother or sister!" Timothy had not learnt that human mummies can only have human babies, and that a mother cat would have to have the kitten – species breed true.

Coloured water

Jason was intrigued when we were talking about coloured solutions. I showed a group of children at school a glass of coloured water (red using food colouring), and challenged them to work out how they could make the colour seem to disappear so that we had a clear solution again.

Jason asked for salt. Our rule in Challenge Science was that if we had the item, they could use it. We didn't tell the learners what equipment and so on they had to use. They had to work out what they thought thy needed to try out their idea for solving a particular challenge. This is all part of the logistics and management of science.

We had salt, and I asked him why he wanted to use it. "Because", he said, "when my mother drops red wine on the carpet she puts salt on it and that takes the red colour away so I think if I add salt to some of the solution it will take out the red." So he tried. He found that this approach did not work with this investigation. He didn't say he had it wrong but that the idea did not work for this but did for the wine on the carpet. Other children worked out that if they kept diluting and diluting the solution it eventually looked as if the colour had disappeared.

Seeds planted to grow a baby

Young children soon understand that seeds grow into new plants. Often at pre-school or home they plant seeds and grow a sunflower, or they have an empty egg shell from a boiled egg with the top removed and place wet cotton wool or similar inside and sprinkle rape and cress seeds on it. They grow the seeds so that the egg shell, on which they draw a face, looks as if it has green hair.

Harriet, the Local Church of England curate's daughter, took her picture book, *New Baby*, which she had been looking at with her mother, who told her that she was going to have a new baby. Harriet planted the book very carefully in the garden, covering it with soil with just a corner peeping out above the soil. She showed her mother and said, "I've planted my new baby book to grow the new baby!" This learner had not yet realised that the act of planting anything did not grow what you wanted.

Magic!

Luc and Josh were sitting at the kitchen table, with a plastic glass of water. We added a spoon of sugar and much of the sugar disappeared. Luc stirred the water and was intrigued as more sugar disappeared. They tried this again with warm water and found more of the sugar disappeared at once. "Magic!" they said!

Walking on water!

Josh was intrigued with the pond in their new garden. There were some animals walking across the water and he couldn't understand how they managed it and didn't sink! We looked very carefully and he noticed that their feet made a small depression on the surface of the water, as if they were skating on a thin layer on top of the water. He was right! This is called the meniscus and very light items do rest on it and do not go under the surface. He was watching insects called pond skaters.

Foundation experiences

Before focusing on the activities suggested, children need to have experience of observing, using measurements, identifying objects and actions and being able to use the required words. They need to be able to manipulate simple equipment and use pencils and crayons and use the Internet for looking up information. They need to be familiar with gardens, planted out but with bare earth, as well as lawns and paved areas, and other outside features and be used to being outside.

Vocabulary

Flowers, fruit, seed, change, young, adult, food, kind, baby, adult, grow up, sift, filter, mix, melt, shadow, dissolve, stir, sieve, ear flap, soak, hard, soft, pour, film, skin, surface, float, sink, heavier, lighter, measure, pour, empty, fill, level, weather, stars, sky, dull, bright, young, grow up, adult, same form, different, gills, pupa, egg, seedling, cook, change, sound, hear, vibrate, chart, germination, germinate, split, root, shoot, cotyledon, cakes, mix, cook, rice, hard, soft, potato, raw, cooked, heat.

You need

Ice water, plastic beakers, candle wax, stick, light source, pictures of day and night, pictures of seasons, seeds, fruits, pine cones, pictures of young, changing and adult stages of animals and plants such as caterpillar, egg, pupa, butterfly, tadpole with external gills, frogspawn changing tadpoles with gill cover, adult frog, tweezers, plastic gloves, trowel, sieves with various sized holes, see-through beaker, pepper, washing up liquid, saucer, a large washing-up bowl, scoop, large spoon, ladle (to measure soil amount), rubber duck, modelling clay, polystyrene balls of various sizes, potato or rice or cake mixture and a cake (uncooked and cooked or pictures thereof), pictures (or real examples) of foods (e.g. apple, banana, cabbage, potato, chips, peas, baked beans, fish fingers, lollipops, milk, sausages, and burgers), cheese, crisps. Photos of puppies and adults, photos of kittens and cats, foals and horses, lamb and sheep, tadpoles and frogs, pictures, models; fast growing seeds; trays or containers in which to soak them; scales; flash card with stages of life cycle and pictures if possible for sequencing or rubber stamps of life cycles; photos of beaches with sand, shingle; pictures of large ships floating, tree floating; yellow circles (to present the sun) and clear sheets of paper, crayons; seeds in pods, e.g. mangetout, broad beans or pictures thereof; plastic beakers or similar to act as a vase in which to put some water and cut flowers; something to measure amounts of water, e.g. a syringe, measuring jug; large spoon for measuring an amount of soil; filter paper/kitchen towel; cut down soft drinks bottles with tops inverted to form funnel.

Aims

Through working with these suggested activities, the learner should begin to understand that many things in their lives, including themselves, change.

- That day and night change from one to the other.
- That weather changes from day to day and that there are different kinds of weather at different times of the year in a regular predictable cycle.
- That living things change as they grow from a baby to a grown up.

- That some living things change their appearance for different times of the year.
- That soil is not the same and other things can change what it looks like.
- Sounds can be made loud and soft.
- Material can change such as diluting coloured water, paper getting wet. Ice melts to water, thus appears to change. Water can be heated; it evaporates and seems to disappear from puddles. Mixtures can be sorted and thus changed. Water does not mix with oil. Raw foods can be cooked.
- Water has a skin.
- Some things float and some things sink.

Activities

Growing up

Changing you

Challenge: "Do you change? What changes?"

What does the learner say? Prompt them. Are they the same size (height particularly) as when a baby. Did they have teeth when they were a baby?

Could they walk then? Do they wear the same clothes as babies? Do they eat the same food? Do they like the same toys? What is different?

"Can you talk about it and find pictures to stick in a book about how you have changed?" Or make a chart and invite them to draw what has changed. You may be able to find pictures from the Internet or magazines to show the changes.

Challenge them: "Can you make up a rhyme about how I changed?"

> When I was a baby I . . .
> Now I am big I . . .
> When I was a baby I . . . but now I am big I . . .

Table 9.1 Me – then and now!

Action	Then	Now
My height		
My speech		
My food		
My clothes		
What I did all day		

Our light

Challenge: "What make the light in our day?"

What do the children say?

Challenge: "Where is the sun in the day?"

What did the children say? How do they know? Where is the sun when it cannot be seen in the sky?

Can they test their idea?

Suggest they may like to draw a picture or take a photograph outside the classroom showing the sky. Mark where the sun is in the sky at the start of the day, middle of the day, and end of the day. Give them a round yellow circle to stick on the paper. What do they find at the end of the day? Is the same result obtained the next day and the next day?

A fixed sun?

Challenge: "Does the sun stay in the same place all day every day or not?" What do the children say? How can they test their idea?

Challenge: "Can you always see the sun in the daytime? Is there always yellow sunlight?"

How can you help the children notice? Make an "Is there sun now?" chart.

Mark the days of the week and morning and afternoon. You could have smiley faces to tick when the sun is out and a dark miserable face for when there is no sun.

Night and day!

Challenge: "How can you tell it is night?"

Ask: "What does day mean to you? What does night mean? How long does night last? Is it always the same length in our country? What happens?"

Table 9.2 The sun chart

Time	Monday	Tuesday	Wednesday	Thursday	Friday
Other weather observations, e.g. rain, clouds in the sky					
Morning					
Afternoon					
What did we find out? Is there a pattern? What colour is the sky in the daytime when the sun is out? When it is not visible? Is that what I thought before I observed?					

The sun

Starting talk: Ask about the sun. When do they see the sun? When the world is dark can they see the sun? When it is night time what can they see in the sky? Is there any light from these?

Challenge: "When can you not see the sun? Why?"

No sun

Challenge: "How do we see things when there is no sunlight?"

Ask: "Is there any light at night? Where is it from? Is it always the same amount?"

The feel of the sun

Challenge: "What does the sun feel like to your hand? To things left in it? How can you find out?"

Choose several items like a metal toy, a piece of paper, a piece of cloth like a towel or T-shirt. Feel them; say what they feel like. Are they hot or cold? Leave them somewhere in the sun for 30 minutes then feel them. Leave them longer; measure the time. What do the items feel like then? Do they all feel the same? What is different? How do they compare to how these things felt, hot or cold, when they were put in the sun to start with?

You can use a lamp to represent the sun when there is no sun!

Difference between night and day

Challenge: "What is the difference between night and day?"

Listen to what the children think are the differences. What do they do at night, in the day?

Night-light

Challenge: "What gives the world light in the day, where is it coming from?"

Ask: "Where is the light at night? Is there light at night? Where from? Where does it come from?

Listen to the learners.

Ask if they can see any light in the sky at night.

What shines at night?

Ask: "What can stop light in the day or night from reaching us?"

What is high in the sky? What is in the air around us?

Challenge: "What is in the sky?"

Ask the learners:

*   What human-made things can we see in the sky?
*   What animals can we see in the sky?

- What plant bits?
- What else is in the sky low down near to us?

Collage – What I have seen in the sky

You may like to make a collage using pictures from magazines or printed off from the Internet of the objects the learners say they can see such as an aeroplane, a bird, a cloud, a hot air balloon, a parachute, a plane with a banner behind, butterfly, a dragonfly, a bee, a fly, a leaf, a seed in the air, litter.

Earth

Orientate children by asking them to look outside. Help them to remember what they see at home and whilst coming to school. If there is not much variation in the local environment, show pictures of a built environment, gardens, and a ploughed field.

Challenge: "What is on the top of the earth? What can you see out of the window?"

What do they notice? You could encourage them to take photographs of differing parts of the outside near you and then talk about the various coverings, tarmac, paving stones, grass lawns, flower beds showing bare earth, for example.

Take photographs and then put them on a table on a large piece of paper, as in column one of Table 9.3, and write what the child says about the photographs and the earth covering for each photograph.

Table 9.3 What is on top of the earth?

Photo I	What it shows	My comments

Covering the earth

Challenge: "What covers the earth when humans have built on it or plants have covered it?"

What is soil like? Are all soils the same?

Inquire what the children already know about soil. What is it? What have they done with it before? What stories can they tell about soil? Collect these for a big book.

Ask them to point out in the pictures or on a walk around school what is natural covering and what humans have made and what is made from plants but humans have put there (lawns, flower bed shapes, buildings, paths). You can put down what the learner says.

What covering has been put there by humans around school and in school (floor)? By nature? What is under the coverings? What is it called? Is it all the same?

Table 9.4 Natural and human-made covering of the earth

Where	What we saw	Its job if any

What is soil?

What is in soil? How can they find out what soil looks like? Look at pictures as well as outside. Suggest you make a big book or a collage of 'Our Soil'. Take photographs of different soils around the garden or the park, or find pictures in magazines and on the Internet.

Ask: "What is covering the earth in some places such as at the seaside? Where vehicles go? Where trains move? How can you find out?"

Garden soil

Challenge: "What does garden soil look like? Look at this soil. What can you see? What words would you say about the soil?"

Make a verbal list. Name the bits.

In my soil I found . . . stamp your feet
In my soil I found. . . . clap your hands (repeat)

Table 9.5 Soil chart

Soil 1	Comment 1	Colour	Looks like	Anything in it? Soil words
Soil 2				

I found a coloured egg green thing
I found a brown thing
I found a . . . . .
I found x number of things!

What do the items look like? Are they the same size? Colour?

Can the learner sort their findings? Give them a large piece of paper and ask them to place the things on it in groups. Which categories will you use? What do they think? Perhaps gather something that is living, such as a leaf, a small non-living thing, such as a pebble, soil, sand, and something that once lived such as a fossil, bit of twig on ground, a dead leaf, or a snail shell.

Dry out!

Challenge: "What happens to the water if you put a small amount out in a dish by the window for a day? Two days? Does it make a difference if the sun shines on the dish or not?"

What do they need? Where do they decide to put their dishes (two are needed exactly the same as a control).

Wet soil

Challenge: "Can you make dry soil wet? How wet?"

What do they think? How can they make this a fair test?

Ask: "How can you measure the same amount of water to see what happens? Why is this important?"

You need a number of different saucers or small plastic beakers, a spoon to measure the soil and something such as a medicine syringe to measure the same amount of water. Cue them to realise how to make their test fair. How will they decide the wetness? Can they notice the colour of the soil when it starts having water added? This is an ideal activity with which to take photographs each time the water is added. Each time add twice as much water as the time before.

Separating things in the soil

Bits in soil

Provide forceps/tweezers or thin plastic bags into which to put their hands so they do not touch the soil with their skin in case of infections. Provide lollipop sticks, spoons or scoops to move the soil around. Garden soil is best.

Challenge: "What are the parts of the soil? What can you find? How can you group the bits?"

Ask: "What did you decide? Size? Colour? Shape? Living, once lived, never lived?" Ask: "Why have you grouped the bits your way?"

Would a grid help? Have a large sheet of plain paper such as computer paper and divide it with straight lines into six squares How could the learner use the grid to sort the sizes of the soil and bits in it?

Table 9.6 Template for soil bits

Bits in the soil	
Smallest	
	Largest

Filter

Have a cut down soda/water bottle with the top cut off and inverted. Take off the cap of the bottle so water can run through into the base of the bottle, put a filter paper, a piece of kitchen towel, a piece from a pair of old tights, stocking, or muslin in the 'funnel'.

Establish that the learner understands what 'to filter' means. Ask if they have an idea of how to make a filter from everyday things. If not, show them one you have made.

Show the setup to the children.

Challenge: "What would happen if you poured some muddy soil into the funnel? What do you think? Why do you say that?"

What happens if they have a towel or cloth over the hole in the funnel? How will they test their idea?

Sieving

Challenge: "How can you separate out the bits in the soil?"

What do they suggest? What apparatus do the children think that they need to do this? Have they seen a sieve?

Perhaps you will be able to look at a kitchen and a garden sieve. Let the children work out how these are used! What action do the children take to make the sieve work? What do they think will happen? Force has to be used to shake the sieve and particles small enough will pass through the holes.

Challenge: "Can you make a sieve from card and paper? What size holes? Why? What happens with big holes? Small holes?"

Ask: "Why don't all the particles of soil pass through the holes?"

Erosion

You need a waterproof covering for the table.

Challenge: "What effect does water have on soil on a slope? How can you find out?"

What are their ideas? How can they make a slope? What do you need to keep one end higher than the other? Provide a waterproof cover and small tray so they can put some soil in it and a small watering can or sprinkler. Where will they pour the water – top, middle or bottom of the slope? After? Pretend it is a hill. Does it make a difference where they pour the water?

Challenge: "How can you stop the water washing away the soil on the slope?"

What do they suggest? Putting lollipop sticks in it to represent trees slows the washing away or erosion of the soil. Ideally, you could have a piece of earth with grass on and a same-sized tray with bare soil and use the same amount of water poured at the same rate from the same utensil in the same place to make this a fair test.

Floating and sinking

Challenge: "What will happen if you put some soil into a container of water?"

Ask: "What shall we use for the water container? How much soil? Does anything float? Sink?"

What is the plan?

What happens?

Challenge: "Are all soils the same in water? What other soils could we try?"

Perhaps they could use sand, gravelly soil, peat or plant compost.

What is the learner's prediction? Why? What happens? You can modify the table above or take photographs of the different soils after they have been added to the water or copy this diagram and have two beakers for each soil they try. Ask them to show the water level then what they think will happen to the soil and what does happen once they have tried the investigation for each soil.

Table 9.7 Floating and sinking soil

Comments – kind of soil	What part of soil floats?	What does not float?

Figure 9.1 A container for water

Other floaters!

Have a fresh bowl of water. What else does the learner want to try to see if it floats or sinks? Have they seen other things float or sink? What happens at bath time?

Using polystyrene balls, one the same size as a rubber ball and a small one the same size as a marble.

Challenge: "What happens to the same-sized balls but made from different kinds of material when you put them in water? What happens to a blown up balloon put into a bowl of water?"

You could photograph the results and make a chart for their prediction and the outcome or use another copy of the container in Figure 9.1.

Alternatively, divide a piece of paper into two with a line horizontally across the paper to represent the surface of the water.

Try out each object the learner has chosen. Ask the learner to tell you what has happened. Then remove the object, dry it and place it on the paper above the water level or below.

Is there a conclusion to what floats and what sinks? What is different about the items? Size? Shape? Mass?

Baby plants

Seeds

Challenge: "Why don't seeds grow in the packet? What do you have to do before they will grow?"

Show the children a pack of seeds, or even a bag of chickpeas, beans or rice grains from the grocery store/supermarket.

Ask: "What are these seeds like? What words can you use to tell me? What shape, size, colour? What do they feel like?"

Ask: "What do you think you could do to get the seeds to grow?"

What do the learners suggest? What do they want to try out?

How much water?

If they suggest water, perhaps because they have seen someone else do this, ask them why they think this is what they should do.

Challenge: "How much water? Will you add water to each seed one by one or to all the seeds at once in the same container and then carefully take the seeds out and put them in separate containers? How would you do that? What is your action plan?"

Ask: "How can you tell if there are changes?" This is an ideal activity to record with a camera.

Will you add water to each seed one by one or to all the seeds at once in the same container and then carefully take the seeds out and put them in separate containers? What happens if they put a lot of water with a seed or the seeds? What happens if they only put a few drops of water for each seed or a group of seeds? How long does the learner think they should wait before looking? How did they record their observations?

Perhaps they could use a chart, which they can fill in with their comments, told to you, and a printout of the photographs.

Talk about seeds

Challenge the learner: "Are the seeds in a packet wet or dry?"

Ask why they gave their answer? What do they know already about seeds?

What have they found out about the needs of the seeds before they will develop? Can they think of why the seeds are dry when they have left their parent and before

 Table 9.8 The changes in a seed

Day	Time	What the seed looks like	Has it changed?	How?	Photographs

they develop when they come into contact with some water? Why do seeds become dry after they leave their parent?

Seed observations

Provide some seeds from a packet such as dried peas or beans. Ask the learner to describe them. Are they hard/soft/size/colour/any marks on the outside?

Challenge: "How many seeds are there? Can you count?"

It may help to have a piece of squared paper with each square numbered to help the learner with their number line and addition.

Challenge: "What do you think happens if we put half the seeds into a beaker of water? Can you count out ten seeds?"

When they have done the activity leave it until the next day, then look with them.

Ask: "Have the seeds changed at all? In what way and which seeds? What do you think has made this happen?"

How much water?

Challenge: "How could you find out how much water the seeds have taken in?"

Ask: "What can we do?"

What are their suggestions? Have a simple balance; put the same-sized container such as a small see-through plastic beaker on each or in each bucket of a beamer balance. Ask the children why. The balance should balance! How can the learner tell that? What does it mean, 'balanced'? Then put the dry seeds in one beaker and put the soaked seeds in the other. What do the children notice? Where has the increased weight come from?

Grow hot or cold?

Challenge: "Will seeds grow in a different temperature?" How can we find out?

What do they think? What investigation do they suggest? How often will they look? How long do they estimate it will take before the seeds start to spout or germinate? How can they tell this process has happened? What do the emergent scientists know a seed needs before it will start growing? Where will they put the seed and container? In the same place as their other seed investigation or place the seed elsewhere? Why do they think this? What is the one thing they are changing to make it a fair test? (Temperature?) Is their plan a fair investigation?

Grow light or dark?

Challenge: "What happens if the seed is put in the dark to grow? Where have the seeds been that you have watched growing? What investigation can you devise?" How is their plan a fair test? What one item is being changed this time? Why?

Starting to grow

Challenge: "What happens to a seed that shows it is beginning to grow and change?"

Table 9.9 Signs of growing

Kind of seed	Wet or dry	What happens to show it is starting to grow?
Day 1		
Day 2		
Day 3		

Ask the learner how they can find out. What do they need to do? How will they keep a record? You could photograph the seed story. If they want to look at different seeds have a table for each kind.

Grow which way up?

Challenge: "Does it matter which way up you plant a seed?"

Ask: "What change happens when a seed grows? What do you know already? Where did you find out? What bits come out of the seed? Do the bits that come out from the seed come out at the same time? What direction do they grow – up or down? Does the same part always grow up, or down?"

What investigation does the learner suggest? How do they make it a fair investigation if they use different kinds of seeds?

Challenge: "What happens if you plant the seeds each lying different ways?"

Ask what they think. How will they test their idea? What do they think a seed needs to grow?

New plants and animals

Babies in a pea pod

Obtain some mangetout or another vegetable that has its fruit pod with the seeds in.

Ask the learner if they know or can work out from where a seed obtains its food whilst developing in the fruit. What makes them say that?

Listen to their ideas. Then open the pod and ask them what they see. They probably notice, for example in mangetout, the same peas forming and attached to the wall of the fruit pod. This is the stalk through which the developing seed obtains its food from the parent plant, similar in function to the umbilical cord of developing mammals, which obtain their food before they are born from their mother's blood through this cord.

Seedlings

If possible obtain a few young plants with no flowers. Perhaps some photographs of seedlings from a plant catalogue could suffice.

Challenge: "Can you tell what kind of plant this is from? What do you see?"

What do they say? It is very difficult to recognise the type of plant seedling until it is in the adult form and producing its characteristic leaves and flowers.

Animal babies

Look alike

Challenge: "Do babies look like their parents when they are born? Do you look like your mother or father or another adult now? What is the same? What is different?"

What does the learner say?

Can they draw an adult shape and their shape and point out the differences such as height, size of head? Grown up men may have beards. Adults wear different clothes.

Match the baby with its mother

Show the learner some farm and zoo animals, which have adult and young models, or show them pictures of the same topic.

Challenge: "Can you match the baby animal to its mother? What reason can you give for your matching?"

Ask if they notice anything. How did they work out which was the baby and which the parent? What is the same? What is different? Why?

Same animal – not lookalike

Show a film clip or photographs of, for example, a blowfly larva and a blow fly, a ladybird larva and a ladybird beetle, a tadpole with gills and an adult frog, a young fish with its egg sac and an adult fish.

Ask the learner to decide what is the same and what is different.

Soak it up!

Challenge: "What happens to a piece of paper if you drop some water on it?"

What do the learners think? Have they had experience of something like this happening? Have they dropped water on their T-shirt, what did it look like before and after? What do they think they could do to see what does happen? Ask them what they need.

Challenge: "Does the same thing happen to all kinds of paper? How could you find out?"

What do they suggest? Ask them how they will make it a fair test. Remind them that everything has to be the same except one thing, the kind of paper that is being tested. How much water will they use each time? How will they make sure it is the same amount? What size of paper will they try? What do they observe? This is their data.

Wet things

Paper colour magic!

Challenge: "What do you think happens if you put a blob of a felt tip pen on a piece of filter paper/kitchen towel and then put that edge of the paper in a small pool of water?"

What will they do to try to find the answers?

Ask: "Does the same thing happen with another coloured felt tip pen? What do you notice? How have you designed your test to make it fair?"

Stopping the wet!

Challenge: "How can you stop the paper becoming wet? What do you wear to stop yourself getting wet in the rain?"

What are their ideas? If they are bemused, provide some white paper and some crayons. Ask if these items could help them solve the challenge. Give another challenge: "What happens if you put water on the paper where you have crayoned part of the paper? Does the water soak into the crayoned part and the non-crayoned part of the paper? How will you find out?"

Skin

Challenge: "Where does water go if you put a drop on your skin?"

What do they think? Talk about it. What can they do to test their idea?

Floating on water?

Challenge: "What do you think happens if you sprinkle pepper on the surface of water?"

What does the learner think? Will the pepper sink or float? Why do they think what they do? How can they try out their explanation?

Ask: "What do you need to investigate this?"

Ask them to draw what they think will happen. You could provide a drawing of a plastic beaker (Figures 9.1 and 2). Ask the emergent scientist to draw in the water and draw the surface of the water (the skin scientifically known as the meniscus) then ask them to draw the pepper floating on top of this surface.

What does the learner think? Why?

Challenge: "What happens if a flower has no water?"

Thirsty flower

Challenge: "Does a flower need water?"

Ask: "What are flowers like when growing in the ground? Do they always stand upright?"

Figure 9.2 A beaker. Fill in water level and the pepper!

See what the learner knows. What do they suggest? How can they make this a fair test?

Sounds around!

Challenge: "What can you hear around you? Listen; tell me three different sounds . . . are they loud or soft sounds? From where do they come?"

Ask them what sound they can make! What part of their body are they using to hear the sound?

Challenge: "Which sound do you like to make the most? How can you make that a softer sound? A louder sound?"

What do they say? How do they plan to make one sound louder then quieter? What do they find out?

Where?

Challenge: "Can you tell where a sound comes from?"

How can we find out?

What sound?

Set up a big book or similar item to act as a screen between you and the learner. Have a collection of everyday items. First of all show them to the learner, then challenge them: "Can you tell which item makes which sound?"

Ask them to sit to one side of the screen and you sit on the other.

One by one make the sound with each of the objects.

Ask: "Did you hear the sound? What was it like – loud, soft? What do you think made that noise?" Keep a record of what they say!

Animal ears

All mammals have ear flaps (except seals!) Show some different mammals.

Challenge: "Are the ears (ear flaps) always in the same place? Are they always the same size?"

What do they say? Ask: "Can you make a list of mammals with big ears, small ears, medium ears?"

Where are the ears?

Show pictures or videos of other animals, such as a kind of bird, a frog, a snake, and an alligator.

Challenge: "Can you find the ears (flaps)?"

What do they do? What do they say?

Moving ears!

Challenge: "Can you move your ear flaps?"

Ask if they have ever seen a mammal moving its ear flaps. Why do they think they do this?

Can you find a video of an animal moving its ear flap? Ask if anyone has seen a dog or a cat moving its ear flaps.

Challenge: "Do big ears make a difference? How could you investigate?"

Help the learner make cones of paper, one very big, and one small. Ask them how they could use these cones to test their idea? What do they think will happen if they listen to the same noise with each cone in turn and then with no cone. Will the noise sound the same or not? Why do they think that? What do they think they will hear? Why? How will they make it a fair test so that only one thing (the size of the cone) is changed?

Plucking!

Give the learner a thick rubber band.

Challenge: "Can you make noises using the rubber band?"

What do they think? What do they do? Why did they do that? Did they make a sound?

Banging!

Provide them with a small box.

Challenge: "Can you make noises using this box? What do you think you can do? Why?"

Watch your learner. What do they do? Ask: "How have you made the sound? Why did you do it that way?"

Cooking change!

Ask: "Do you eat food raw or cooked? What raw things do you eat? What cooked things?"

Find pictures of foods, some of which we eat cooked like meat and some raw like apples.

Cut out the pictures. Prepare a chart and invite the learner with you to place the foods in the cooked or uncooked columns.

Show the learner a small amount of uncooked rice. Ask them if they know what it is and what it is used for. Then show them some cooked rice. Ask them what has happened. Can they describe the change? So what has changed the uncooked rice? Do they know?

If they are unfamiliar with rice show them pictures of a raw egg (or a real one broken into a dish) and then of a cooked fried egg (or a hardboiled egg with half the shell removed). Has the learner seen a cooked egg? How are they cooked?

They may have experienced cakes or you may even do some baking with them. If not, show them a picture from a cookbook or the Internet of a bowl with the ingredients being mixed and then show them a picture of the end result – fairy cakes, perhaps. Ask them how the ingredients changed into the fairy cakes. What do they think happened? What does the cook do to the mixture to change it into a cake?

Table 9.10 Food I eat cooked and uncooked

I eat this food uncooked (raw).	I eat this food cooked.

Can they reply that it has to be cooked? Do they know what cooking is, heat? If you have a play area with a cooker etc., or at home in the kitchen, you can act out the process of cooking. Encourage your learner to talk about what they are doing as they pretend to cook.

Challenge: "What did we need to do to cook the cakes?

What did they say?

Assessment

Keep a record of the questions and answers children give to your questions for selected activities. Photograph them carrying out procedures and make notes on differing aspects of inquiry.

What floats?

Provide a selection of small items, some of which will float and some sink. Invite the children to place them on a piece of paper one by one. Use paper with a line drawn across horizontally to represent the surface of the water. Ask the learner why s/he has placed the object where s/he has and why.

Note their responses.

This should reveal an understanding of mass and density.

Germination

Show them some dried peas and some soaked peas. Ask them what is different and why they think this has happened. Their answers should reveal whether they understood the relevant activity.

Provide them with an empty tin and a full tin of the same size and label (peas, baked beans). Alternatively, provide two glasses or mugs of the same size, one with water and one without or two bottles, and a metal teaspoon. Ask them what will happen when they strike the tins. Do they know the difference between the two tins that could explain what they find out? What happens if you use a plastic spoon instead of a metal one? Can they tell you? Why?

Hearing

Have some pictures of animals without ear flaps: a bird, a lizard or snake or crocodile, a frog. Ask them which animal in the pictures has ear flaps. What are they used for?

Magnets

Provide a magnet and some objects that are wrapped up, e.g. paper clip, plastic comb, safety pin, sweet, ball of foil, crayon.

Ask the learner how they can find out which are magnetic and which objects are not.

Fill in the appropriate record and assessment charts.

Outcomes

Through thinking and doing the activities about change learners should:

- Realise that different types of soil have simple but different properties of appearance and water retention.
- Use appropriate vocabulary to talk about what they do and observe.
- Be able to manipulate and observe different soils.
- Collaborate and share observations with other children.
- Carry out simple filtration.
- Establish a fair test concept with the help and support of the teacher.

Chapter 10

Outside

Background

This chapter focuses on environmental education with the purpose of developing knowledge and understanding, as well as shapes, space and measure and basic science. It can also serve as education about the environment with the issue of litter and waste disposal being highlighted. We humans live in a world that has been altered from the natural state, as through various activities we have changed the way much of it looks. For example, roads cover the earth as well as pavements and buildings constructed from various available materials such as wood, plastic, stone, steel and glass. These buildings serve different functions such as homes, shops, places of worship, places of recreation, such as sports grounds and theatres, and places that help, such as hospitals, fire stations and schools. Where there are no buildings there are open spaces. These may be parks, gardens or allotments and some parts may be left as vegetation. Away from built-up areas there may be woods or fields for agriculture, fields for crops and livestock as well as wild areas such as moorland and woods. Children may notice the changes in vegetation as days and year progress, including seed growing, which is an activity in an earlier chapter. They may notice changes in the form of animals from young to adult, complete changes in form, complete metamorphosis or notice the gradual changes in humans. The outside is where we use different means of transport for people and goods, ranging from vehicles on roads, railways and waterways, as well as land used for airports or docks by the sea. Vehicles require something, a force, to make them go, usually a push from a motor or enough force, such as wind.

Streets, parks and playgrounds, including school grounds and their playgrounds, have furniture, such as benches, climbing frames, slides, waste bins, goal posts, as well as hard human-made surfaces, linking with materials. Different parts of the outside of schools have different functions such as a drive, parking area for vehicles, playground, paths, gardens, possibly a playing field, perhaps a pond and a nature area. Streets, too, have different parts. Often walls or the side of the roads have signs and there may be pavements alongside the roadways into and around the school buildings. Buildings and outside public furniture, such as signs, seats, post boxes and lamp posts are made of shapes, which the children can identify. Using the school as a reference point, children can work out the direction from these outside features and ways to reach them, hence applying knowledge of space and position. Conducting surveys also enables children to practise their data handling and interlineation abilities.

Children's ideas

Children have to work out the differences between the inside and the outside. These scenarios, from real life, illustrate how children can experience phenomena every day and engage in active investigations and consider consequences that their actions can bring by using their experiences and curiosity.

Lights on!

Jessica could not understand why when outside, towards the end of an afternoon, the light began to fade, requiring inside lights to be put on, so she could see better.

Changing plants

Alan, when a toddler, was intrigued that the greenish tips on top of the plant stems in a row of tulips alongside a path in the garden, had changed into pink flowers with individual parts. He found that he could pull off each bit (petal) until there were none left at the end of each stalk. This self-imposed task took him some time to complete, nonetheless he was very pleased with his achievement in making the plants change back to green again.

Time to grow

Luc planted some seeds with his grandmother; he knew that seeds grow into bigger plants with flowers. He'd seen that on the television, that seeds could grow into sunflowers! Next day he rushed to see the plant pot. No plants. He was so upset. The concept of lapsed time, from planting to germination and the plant appearing above the ground, was new to him.

Push for action!

Luc knew about pushing on the ground with his feet to make his little wooden tricycle move. He pushed hard and worked up speed but found that this was far more difficult on grass and gravel surfaces, but much easier on the smooth surface of the driveway. He experienced friction. However, when presented with a tricycle with pedals and a chain, he could not make the vehicle move. He just could not work out how to push down on the pedal, not the floor, to go forward. He became very frustrated, and even when shown, could not master this new technique to push down to propel the bike forward!

Brick lines

Angus, for some reason when a toddler, was intrigued by the lines between bricks and tried to colour them in with coloured crayons; purple was his favourite.

Stop and go!

Alan sat in the front of the car, which was parked on a slope. The car doors had been left ajar as the car sat stationary. He liked pulling and pushing things and managed to release the handbrake and was delighted when the car rolled forward down the gentle slope! Not much damage was done, a bush stopped the car.

Windmill turn

At a carnival stall, 3-year-old Thaj was bought a windmill on a stick; the stall had a fan and unbeknown to Thaj, this fan created a draft, which caused the 'windmills' to turn.

She was very excited at being given a windmill on a stick but burst into tears because her windmill did not turn; it was static. Her mum had to blow and show her that the blades needed a force, a wind of some sort, to make the windmill turn. After that she was happy, exerting much energy in blowing!

Raindrops

Daniel was interested in the raindrops on the window and watched them running down. It was very heavy rain, and he couldn't work out why the raindrops were not inside.

Change the channel

Whilst at the zoo, a little girl I saw was inspecting the aquarium exhibit with a wooden framed window. The girl announced that she was bored and she wondered where the switch was to change the channel, so she could look at another view!

Aims of activities

These activities are designed to help the learner be aware of:

- their environment;
- the difference between inside a building and outside it;
- what furniture there is inside and outside;
- what floor coverings there are and what they do;
- the direction that things are coming from where the child is;
- changes in living things, a day and seasons;
- changes inside and outside from pushes and pulls;
- practising the recognition of shapes in the environment;
- some data collecting and interpretation.

Foundation experiences

The learners should be able to use the words about shape, space and measure and be able to carry out simple processes like measuring quantities such as temperature, length, and know positional words and their meanings. They should experience the difference between inside and outside and be able to talk about it and what it means to them.

They should have been in the locality and have had experience of streets and the various buildings and layout of the neighbourhood where they live and where their school is located. They should be able to recognise items of furniture inside and outside and know how they are used.

Vocabulary

Direction, rubbish, waste, pavement, road, building, door, window, glass, roof, furniture, vehicle, shadows, transport, change, inside, outside, view, sign, names of the main plants and animals that you can see from the classroom, puddle.

You need

Photographs or images on a tablet or similar of views outside from your learning area and their views of the outside of school. Prepare an outline of the classroom and of the area outside the classroom (to let the learner draw the furniture). You will need: paper, scissors, pictures or examples of clothes for different weather, pieces of plastic gutter, a brick, a piece of wood (or pictures of building materials, cut out shapes, pictures of different types of buildings, fresh and dried leaves and leaf skeletons or pictures thereof), dried seed heads, the flower and pictures of them, twigs, pebbles, some soil in a plastic cup. Also prepare pictures of vehicles, including bicycles, cars and lorries. Cut out footprint shapes (from newspaper perhaps). Have a map to show the local area layout of streets and parks, a timer, thermometer and lamp or torch.

Activities

Outside shapes and space

I spy shapes challenge: "I spy a white oblong square shape on the wall? What do I spy?"

Explain that they have to look around the room and see if they can recognise something with the shape and colour you describe.

Hunt for some other things in your classroom, such as door knobs (round and shiny). Look for different shapes and colours in the classroom, such as oblongs (children's desks) or round black and white items (clock).

Your turn?

Challenge: "Can you choose something for me to guess? Tell me about it but not its name!"

Ask the children perhaps to find a shape first, then a coloured item.

Positional I spy!

Once the learners understand the idea of the game, suggest that next time, they will extend this game by playing "Positional I spy". Children might describe the position of an item using positional language, such as inside, outside, above, below, next to and so on. The classroom practitioner should model the game, starting the game by saying,

"I spy with my little eye, behind me a square object that is larger than the seat of your chair. Where is it?" (A window pane or something similar.) Alternatively, you could say "I spy with my little eye a round item above you." (Perhaps a round lampshade.)

Hot and cold walk

Challenge: "Does everything in the room feel the same hotness or coldness as we do? How can we find out?" Instruct the learners to touch their hand with their other hand and ask, "What does it feel like?"

What do children suggest about how to find out what the items in the classroom feel like compared with themselves? Go on a hot/cold walk around the class touching different surfaces and then describing them orally. Suggest they test an item and describe their finding, such as, "This is smooth and feels cooler than me" (e.g. a plastic chair or tray).

Ask: "How can we record what we find out?"

Suggest that they look round and choose what they will test first of all. Make a record sheet as they notice differences in temperature. Children could use a table with two columns, one labelled "Hotter than me" and the other labelled "Cooler than me". You could cut out from a catalogue pictures of items in the classroom that you have tested and stick them on the chart in preparation.

The child could be given a shape of red sticky paper and a blue shape, stars are popular, and stick the appropriate colour on the chart for 'hotter than' or 'colder than'.

What did the children find out? Did they all have the same results or were there differences in their findings? How can they tell which temperature, hot or cold, is felt most often?

 Table 10.1 "Hotter than, colder than" chart

Item	Hotter than me to touch	Cooler than me to touch
Door handle		
Chair seat		
Table top		
Wall		
Book		
Paper towel		
Pen		
Outside window pane		
Coat		
Bottle of cold water (with top on)		
Total		

Table 10.2 I see shapes!

Shape	Is it in our room?	Where?
Square		
Circle		
Rectangle		
Hexagon		
Triangle		
Oval		
Semicircle		
Cylinder		
Cube		
Total		

Count the shapes?

Challenge: "How many square things can we see in our room? How can we find out? How can we record this?"

What do they suggest? A chart perhaps made with shapes stuck down the side?

Ask: "How do we know how many of this shape we have seen?"

Outside shapes

Challenge: "What shapes can you see outside from our window? How can you record them?"

Ask the learner what they can do to answer your challenge. What do they say? This is an observation and recording activity and useful for assessment. Can the learner recognise shapes in the various items outside? Ask children what shapes the items are (such as a climbing frame). What different shapes can you see in the items?

Floor shapes

Challenge: "What shapes cover the floor inside? How can you find out? Which shape is the one seen most often? How can you tell?"

Look at the floor in your classroom. Name what you see. What is its base shape? How can these observations be recorded?

What is the first floor covering? Carpet? Tiles? How many things cover the floor?

Shapes on the ground

Walk on a pre-planned path around the school in order to explore the shapes on the floor and ground and the walls of the building.

Challenge: "What shapes can you see? Is there one seen most often? How can you tell?"

Ask: "Are there more shapes on walls of buildings than there are covering the ground? How could you find out?"

What is their plan?

What do they find out? Ask: "What are the most common shapes seen?"

Shapes on buildings

Taking photographs with a tablet or camera is a useful way of recording the outside shapes. Do your learners suggest this way of recording?

Show children different charts that could record their data (e.g. a pictogram or bar chart). This activity could utilise the computer to illustrate data handling. Otherwise, show children squared paper and ask how they could set out their findings.

Ask: "What is the shape seen the most outside on buildings? Why?"

Shapes in nature

Challenge: "Are there any shapes in nature that you can identify?" Perhaps card outlines of shapes can be held up to the naturally occurring objects and can be provided if the child has problems recognising the shapes. This will help children see the nearest fit.

Ask: "What is the shape you see most often? Is it in clouds or trees or other plants?"

Shape walk

Go outside the learning area, around the rest of the building and look for shapes. You could make a "shape seen" chart like the one in Table 10.2. If you have several learners, allocate different roles: one child could record, another child could be the timekeeper and the other children the observers. Provide a clipboard for the recorder. Ask how they will note what is seen.

Back after the walk

Provide some large squared paper. When you have counted up the number of shapes let the children colour in a column to show how many items of each shape they found. The different shapes can be drawn under the x axis to show the different shapes and the aligned columns. Children should colour one square to represent one shape. Then repeat for another shape. They will have constructed a bar chart, a simple visual representation of data. This is also an excellent activity to introduce mathematical language related to charts, such as the x and y axis and the meaning of data and how we can represent it.

When a number of shapes have been recorded ask the children: "Which was the shape most often seen? Which shape was not seen? Which was not seen much?" They will be explaining and interpreting their data.

Sticking shapes

Some children might prefer to have a stack of cut-out paper shapes, which could be stuck on the recording sheet. You may be lucky enough to have ink stamps with different shapes, which children enjoy using to make a mark on the recording sheet.

Repeat for outdoors. Compare the charts inside and outside for the shapes.

Ask: "Which shape is seen mostly inside? Which shape is seen mostly outside? How can you tell? Which is the least seen? Is that the same finding inside as it is outside? How do you know?"

Bird's-eye view – maps

Challenge: "What do you think are the main furniture and fittings (like windows, bookshelves, sand tray) in our classroom? How could you explain what and where the main things in our room are?"

What does the learner suggest? Perhaps they say to take a photo?

Compose a scenario where the information has to be sent to someone who has no email, no computer, no telephone and has to receive the information by postal mail. What do they suggest?

Ask: "What do you see if you look down onto something like the model farm or other items that are in the learning area? Does it look the same as when you look from the side? What is different? Why?" Encourage children to use positional language.

Perhaps you have a play mat with a town scene. Look at that to establish that it is a bird's-eye view or show them something similar.

Ask children if they can first of all make a model of an area in their classroom. Children can make a model using wooden bricks or other objects of their choice; allow children to choose which layout in the room they are going to construct. If available, you could use a doll's house and children could pick a room to base their model on.

Ask: "Is this 2D or 3D? How could we turn this information into 2D information on the computer or a piece of paper?" What do they suggest?

Rubbish

Where does rubbish go?

Challenge: " Where do you put litter, waste and rubbish at school? How can you reach the waste bin in your room from where you are working now?"

Rubbish count

Challenge: "What kind of rubbish do we throw away in our classroom? How can you find out?"

What does the learner suggest? Perhaps they sit by the bin for a definite period of time, which can be timed by a stopwatch or a minute timer. You could have a volunteer timer expert (responsible for turning the minute timer for a duration of perhaps five minutes) with a clipboard and they could tick every time someone comes to place something in the bin.

After a time you may empty the contents onto an area of protective cover. Identify what has been disposed.

Other "rubbish" questions require observation and research.

- "Who puts rubbish in the bin in class?"
- "Who empties the class bin?"
- "Who puts things in the big bins?"
- "Who empties the large school bins?"
- "Where does the rubbish go?"

Challenge them to find out. What do they suggest?

Talk about why we need to look after rubbish and throw it away in special places.

Bins

Challenge: "Where does rubbish go?"

Ask: "Can you find out?" What ideas do they have?

As a prompt, ask: "Are they in front of the building? Behind? At the side? Where are bins at other places you go?"

Ask: "What are the bins made from? What shape are they? Which shape do you prefer? Why?"

Which way?

Cut out some paper/card footsteps and put them on the floor from a starting point and to an end point. Let the learner lay out a route they take. Make a template out of card and then cut some footprints out of newspaper so there is a pile available.

Challenge: "Can you design and make a footprint route for others to follow? Where will you go?"

Describe the routes taken. You may prefer to stick the footprints down with double-sided tape. Ask the children what other ways they know of following a path or trail. What other ways could you help people around the outside of your school? What would you like them to see? Choose one thing, e.g. the pond, the log pile, the climbing frame. Decide how you would show someone the way. (Suggestions include making a computer concept keyboard overlay, drawing a pictogram, taking a photograph.)

Trails

Follow a trail

Design a trail around where you are with simple instructions with pictures of items, such as clock, a computer, bookshelves, benches, a potted plant. Have pictures that the children can recognise. Have them arranged on a card in the order in which they will be seen in the room or wherever you choose to make the trail.

Challenge: "Can you follow the trial and notice one thing at each place or where it is? Can you explain what you notice and its location? What sort of words will you need to use?"

Can they follow the trail? What do they say?

Outside trail

Compose another trail around the outside of the school. Have, for example, a door, a sign, a flowerbed, a waste bin, and a bench.

Can the learner follow your trail? Perhaps you could put out small items, like a small figure, in each place where they are expected to find an item and they can bring back the items to the classroom to show they followed the trail.

Nature trail

You may already have a nature trail. Write and print out a simple nature trail for the learner. Use drawings or photographs of the objects so they can identify them and thus follow the trail. Give them a sticker to put on when they have reached an object on the trail. Features might include a blade of grass, a tree, a stone, a plant pot.

Treasure hunt

Tell them to bring something back such as a blade of grass, leaf from the ground, a leaf skeleton, a twig and a pebble and explain from where they obtained it.

Ask: "What do the leaves show?" (If possible, show children leaves in different cycles of life, i.e. a fresh leaf and a dried leaf or a leaf skeleton.)

Change – materials

Built of what?

Walk outside your building.

Challenge: "What is it made of? How many different materials?"

Identify the range of materials (e.g. brick wall, roof tiles, wooden/plastic window frame or glass windows) then make a table for the children to fill in showing what the constituent parts are made from. This activity can be supported by using photographs to show items, such as the gutter of a house.

Table 10.3 What the building is made from?

Part of building	What this part does	This is made of . . .?

After identifying the materials from which things are made discuss which appear natural and which are man-made (e.g. man-made glass or bricks (from natural material), plastic guttering or wooden frames).

Challenge: "How would you sort out those materials that are human made and which are made from natural things?"

What does the learner suggest? What do they plan to do? Sets? Are sets based on colour or shape? Do they know the name for any of the items?

Discussion could develop into how natural materials are processed for building and how building materials are manufactured. Which of the materials do the children like? Why?

Are the buildings nearby made of the same materials?

Weather

Weather effects

Does the weather change?

Challenge: "How can you record the weather changes?"

Using or designing and making a weather board could record the weather for a short time, or making a diary as a big book, a zigzag book or similar could be a technology activity with the children discussing the need to record and designing how they are going to do this.

The sun

Ask: "Where is the sun? How can you tell?"

Peek a boo sun!

Challenge: "How can you tell if the sun is not hidden by clouds in the daytime?" What do the learners say?

Ask: "How often is the sun shining in one day?"

How can the learner keep a record? How many times will they record whether the sun is out or not? How?

Equal time?

Challenge: "Is the sun out the same amount every day? How can you find out?"

Sun and heat

Challenge: "Are you able to tell, from looking outside, the effect of the sun on things?"

What do the children say? Ask what happens if something is in the way of the light from the sun.

Ask: "Have you noticed shadows? Where? When? Are they always there?"

If they are not aware of shadows you could demonstrate by using a lamp or torch and shine the beam at a wall, then place different objects in front of the beam and ask the children to notice what has changed.

Then ask, "How can you tell the light is shining? What happens to the light on the wall if something is on the wall?"

This activity can lead to making shadow puppets and making a story!

Sun effect

Challenge: "What happens if you leave something in the sun or under a lamp with its light on?"

How can the learner make an investigation to test their idea? How will they make it a fair test? What will be their control? What is the thing that is altered?

Ask the children what they will use to test and how will they have a control (i.e. make it a fair test)? How will they assess the temperature? A thermostick thermometer could be used or the skin of your hand for a rough estimate.

Puddles!

When are there puddles?

Challenge: "What is a puddle? Where can you see them? When can you see them?"

Listen to what they say. What have they noticed? Is there a rhyme about puddles? There is this traditional nursery rhyme:

Dr Foster, went to Gloucester
In a shower of rain.
He stepped in puddle, right up to his middle
And never went there again.

Ask what it means. Draw a picture of the doctor in the puddle!

Ask: "Where is his middle? Was it a shallow or deep puddle? How can you tell? What are the puddles like that you see?"

Can the child act out the story of the doctor and the puddle?

Ask: "What happens when you walk in a puddle?"

Disappearing puddles

Challenge: "What happens to a puddle? Does it stay there always?"

What does the learner say? Have they noticed puddles? When do you see puddles?

Challenge: "How can you investigate if a puddle goes away?"

What do they suggest?

This needs to be done after rain or make a puddle in a small depression in a path and draw a line around it in chalk, around its circumference. Does the learner suggest this? If so, why? If not, ask them why you are recording this. Decide with the learner/s when you are going to check the size of the puddle again. How else, besides seeing if the circumference decreases, could you tell if the puddle is becoming smaller? It may be changing another dimension, such as depth.

Can the learner explain why this has happened?

Puddle weather

It is useful to make a note of the weather, for instance, is it windy or is the sun shining after you have made the puddle? Ask the learner why this information is important in this investigation. This activity could be supported by looking at the water cycle or watching video clips available on the Internet.

Walls and floors

Wall direction – inside and outside

Challenge: Point to the walls. "What are these? What is their job? What are they made from? What is on them? How many are there? Where are they from you?"

This is an assessment tool as it revises simple directional words such as front, back, left and right.

Look at the floor and ask what it is. Where is it (revising the simple directional words such as down, next).

Coloured walls

Challenge: "Are walls the same colour?"

What do the children think? How could they test their idea (hypothesis)? Which coloured wall do they like to be near? Why?

Covering walls

Challenge: "How many different kinds of things are on the walls? How could you find out?" Perhaps they might suggest a survey with a large chart with a picture for each group of items (e.g. pictures, display board, windows) per wall.

Floor things

Challenge: "What is on the floors? How many different things? How can you find out and keep a record?"

Ask: "Do all the rooms we go in have the same kind of floor covering? How many different kinds of floor covering can you find (e.g. tiles, carpet, woodblocks)?"

Ask: "Why do floors have different kinds of covering? What effect does the covering have? What coverings are put where? Why?"

Sounds around

Sound surveyor

Challenge: "How many different sounds can you hear in the room? How can you keep a record?"

What do they suggest? For how long will they listen? How will they time the listening time? Will they make a tally chart? You could act as recorder by writing the name of the sound.

Table 10.4 Outside sounds

Noise	Heard	Total	Not heard	Total
Birds				
Other animals				
Children				
Aeroplanes				
Cars				
Machines				
Wind blowing				
Sound not heard at all				
Sound most heard				

Outside sound

Challenge: "Are there sounds you can hear outside? What do you think you will hear? How can you find out?"

What investigation do they suggest to observe what sounds are outside?

Perhaps a tally chart sheet will assist this activity with either you or a child within the group acting as the recorder. First make a list of what they think they may hear. Leave rows in the chart for other sounds.

Ask: "Which sound is heard the most in the listening time? How long did you listen? How do you know?"

Outside furniture

Challenge: "What furniture is in your playground or garden? What do you like best?"

Walk around the school grounds, especially the playground. Talk about each item the children point out.

Ask: "What kind of furniture do you see on streets? Shall we make a list and find pictures of them to make a chart?

Table 10.5 Things in the street

Item	Where seen	What is it for?	Comments
E.g. post box	At the corner of the road on the pavement	Posting letters	It is red

What do the children recall? A post box? Bus stop? Waste bin? Bench? Bicycle stand? Signs? Traffic lights? Things from shops on the pavement? Plant pots?

When they have remembered all they can, ask for each item; guide children to describe the item and its purpose by asking: "What is it? Where is it? What is it for? What shape is it? What is it made from?"

Nearby

Look out of a window or doors at the front of your building.

Challenge: "What can you see outside our building?"

Ask the child to describe the scene. What things are familiar? It may be the type of shops or a telephone kiosk. What is different about the picture compared with the street; nearest home or school?

It may be that the school is in the country and there are no shops down the street; or it may be in the middle of a town and there are no residential houses, only offices and shops.

Vehicle count

Begin this activity by taking a survey of how the children in the class travel to school.

Challenge: "How many vehicles come to your school in a day? How could you find out?"

What is suggested?

Perhaps you could use stickers in different shapes to represent different kinds of vehicles, a circle for cars, a star for vans and so on. Which shape do the learners choose when they have seen how many of each kind passes? Can they make a bar chart with them?

Table 10.6 Passing vehicle chart

Kind of vehicle	Tick or tally	Total
Car		
Van		
Lorry		
Bicycle		
Motorbike		
Bus		
Scooter		
Other		

Ask the children if they know of the different types of vehicle that might visit the school. This might include motorbikes, cars, vans, lorries or refuse collection vehicles.

Passing by

If the situation is suitable, you could suggest that the learners undertake a survey, recording (a tally chart is ideal) the different vehicles visiting the school by inspecting the car park or surveying the nearest street to the school to count the different kinds of vehicles passing and their frequency. Use sticky circles again for children who are not used to tallying with a mark.

Which vehicle is their favourite ? Why? Can they draw it?

Colours of vehicles – reading data!

Challenge: "Are all the vehicles the same colour?"

What do they say? Why do they say that?

Table 10.7 Colours of car

White	Red	Black	Green	Blue	Silver	Gold	Tally or tick	Total

Replace these with the appropriate words for whatever is being counted.

Perhaps they can colour the chart or stick a small sticky star or circle for the colour of each vehicle of one kind that they see and then add up when they have finished, colouring the number of marks they made if they cannot yet tally. Choose a car first. Then they can count perhaps vans, then buses, or the bricks they build things with if they are different colours, or Lego bricks of a certain shape. In that case you may have to alter the colours used on the chart. What can the learner tell you about the numbers of vehicles in the same colour? Can they point to their chart and explain?

Challenge: "What does your chart tell you?"

Which kind of vehicle interests the learner most? Why do they say that?

Assessment

Many of these activities consolidate experiences from the previous chapters so the responses of the learners serve as a form of summative assessment, if carried out after the other content of chapters. If you have activities to fit in with other work, use the assessment sheets suggested for all the changes.

Fill in the relevant assessment and recording charts if applicable.

Summary

Carrying out some of the investigations and joining in dialogue, the learner should:

- Be aware of the environment that is made of natural things and things constructed by humans.
- Have an introductory understanding of the difference between inside a building and outside of it.
- Be aware of the different size and shape of buildings and the differing parts of them and the things inside and outside of them.
- Recognise street furniture.
- Be aware of rubbish and the need for disposal.
- Understand and experience some use of signs and directions.
- Appreciate that the 'outside' changes more than the 'inside'.
- Recognise changes in the outside suited to the passage of time and the daily fluctuations in weather.
- Be able to construct simple tally charts and interpret simple bar charts.

Index